# This Soldier Life

The Diaries of
Romine H. Ostrander,
1863 and 1865, in Colorado Territory

Annotated by

## Paul A. Malkoski

COLORADO HISTORICAL SOCIETY

*Colorado History*

ISSN 1091-7438

Number 13
2006

## COLORADO HISTORICAL SOCIETY
Research and Publications Office

*Managing Editor*
Steve Grinstead

*Editor*
Ben Fogelberg

*Chief Historian*
Modupe Labode

*Graphic Designer*
Susan Romansky

*Volume Editors*
Larry Borowsky and David N. Wetzel

COVER: *Fort Lyon*, 1936, Robert Lindneux. Colorado Historical Society. 10031783

The Colorado Historical Society publishes *Colorado History* to provide a flexible scholarly forum for well-written, documented manuscripts on the history of Colorado and the Rocky Mountain West. Its twofold structure is designed to accommodate article-length manuscripts in the traditional journal style and longer, book-length works which appear as monographs within the series. The publications of the Society generally follow the principles and conventions of the *Chicago Manual of Style*, and an author's guide is available on request. Manuscripts and letters should be addressed to: Research and Publications Office, Colorado Historical Society, 1300 Broadway, Denver CO 80203. The Society disclaims responsibility for statements of fact or opinion made by contributors.

Generous assistance from Giles D. Toll has helped make this publication possible.

# Contents

# Preface

Diaries of the common man represent exceptional historical gems; diaries of Civil War–era enlisted men in Colorado stand out even more. Charles E. Vest discovered the diaries of Romine Ostrander in 1922 in the Eagle Warehouse in Fresno, California; it is unclear how they got there. They hold the daily observations of one Pvt. Romine H. Ostrander of the Colorado First Cavalry from 1863 and 1865 and afford a unique glimpse at military and frontier life during Colorado's somewhat shaky beginnings.

Born in 1837, Ostrander hailed from Roseville, Illinois, but no one knows how he came to Colorado or into the army, though he may have enlisted at the beginning of the Civil War. On February 26, 1863, he acquired his first 3½ x 5–inch leather-bound journal in which he recorded, in a clear, steady hand in pencil, his daily thoughts, travels, frustrations, and observations for the next ten months. He apparently maintained a diary for 1864, which is now lost, and another in 1865. The two delicate, well-worn volumes accompanied the private in his saddlebags over miles of dusty Colorado trails. Given the conditions of the time, it is remarkable that they survived at all.

In his 1863 volume, which he purchased in late February, Ostrander crossed out the unused dates from January 1 to February 25 and recorded there his reminiscences of his adventures as part of Col. John C. Slough's Colorado troops, which defeated Confederate raiders under Lt. Col. William R. Scurry at Glorieta Pass in what is now northern New Mexico. Ostrander went on write about the boredom and tedium that earmarked most of his days as he fulfilled rather menial duties that included guarding horse herds, fetching water, or attending to the sick in Camp Weld's infirmary. When at home in Camp Weld, near Denver, he and his comrades passed much of their time sleeping or gambling, carousing, and sometimes getting into fights. Hardly the romantic stuff of legend or movies. Yet in April 1863, just one year after Glorieta Pass and still indicating his concern for possible rebel raiders, Ostrander was part of a detail of soldiers that traveled to Fairplay to protect citizens from what he thought were Confederate guerrillas, but who actually were the marauding Espinosa brothers. In August 1863, he recounts an uneventful patrol from Denver into northeastern Colorado and southeastern Wyoming, remarkable if for no other reason than the distances traveled, usually between forty and fifty-five miles a day on horseback, often living off the land.

More intriguing for the modern reader might be Ostrander's omissions. When the attacks and killings near Fairplay ended in May 1863, did Ostrander know that the perpetrators were none other than the "bloody Espinosas," who killed an estimated thirty Anglo men on their vendetta-driven rampage? He never mentions them by name, even after the legendary mountain man Tom Tobin tracked and killed Filipé and his nephew José some five months later. Was Ostrander not interested or unaware? Months later, in his entry on January 24, 1865, he makes clear his feelings regarding the soldiers who attacked the Cheyennes and Arapahos at Sand Creek on November 29, 1864 (he calls them murderers of defenseless women and children). Yet three months later, he fails to mention Lincoln's assassination, even though the *Rocky Mountain News* reported the sad story on April 17, two days after it occurred. Surely Ostrander, the self-confessed Union and Lincoln man (June 2, 1863), must have reacted to the news. Why were his mundane daily comings and goings more worthy of a diary entry? Would the missing 1864 diary contain entries about the infamous Reynolds Gang or the Sand Creek Massacre, or did Ostrander ignore those events as well?

After Ostrander left the army in late 1865, he tried his luck cutting timber in the foothills near Denver. A search of Denver business directories revealed that he worked as a teamster at Hartman's stable in 1872, then as a policeman in 1873, a fact corroborated by an item in the *Rocky Mountain News*, February 7, 1873, as reported in *Hell's Belles: Prostitution, Vice, and Crime in Early Denver* by Clark Secrest. The business directory listed him as a farmer in 1874. There are no further entries for him after that date.

A few comments on the main text and the publication team are in order. No publication is a solitary effort, and this is no exception. Ed Ellis, president of the Volunteers of the Colorado Historical Society, spent untold hours diligently transcribing Ostrander's entries, preserving his spellings, syntax, and grammar, all of which appear here almost entirely uncorrected in an effort to preserve the texture and feel of the original. An occasional period has been added for readability. Colorado historians Tom Noel and William J. Convery III combed the text and footnotes for accuracy and made important recommendations. Ovando J. Hollister's *Boldly They Rode: A History of the First Colorado Regiment of Volunteers* proved invaluable because it includes a complete roster of the names and rank of the unit's 963 men as of February 28, 1863, thus allowing for the identification of most of the soldiers mentioned in the journals.

Like so many primary sources, Ostrander's diaries leave us yearning for more, wishing for added detail and greater insight into the man, his background, and his thoughts. Perhaps his 1864 diary will appear some day, but just knowing that it existed intrigues us all the more. After all, some of our fascination with history comes in not knowing.

# Ostrander's 1863 Itinerary

| 1863 | Destination | Mileage |
|------|-------------|---------|
| April 4 | Denver to Cobley's Ranch | 37 miles |
| April 7 | To Colorado City | 33 miles |
| April 8 | To California Ranch on Cherry Creek | 50 miles |
| April 9 | Returns to Denver—mentions guerillas for the first time | |
| April 15 | Leaves Denver for Bradford's Ranch | 15 miles |
| April 16 | Tarryall Road to mountains | 30 miles |
| April 17 | To Kenosha House | 20 miles |
| April 18 | To South Park | 5 miles |
| | Leaves Tarryall Road | 3 miles |
| | To Fairplay | 25 miles |
| April 19 | Joins detail with five days rations to Cañon City on trail of guerillas | 15 miles |
| | Continues traveling—no mileage recorded— to Buffalo Springs | |
| April 20 | Travels to head of Trout Creek | 15 miles |
| April 21 | Travels down Trout Creek to the Arkansas, then down to Brownville; returns to Trout Creek | 35 miles |
| April 22 | Goes into South Park, then to Weston's Ranch, then to Fairplay | 58 miles |
| | Leaves Guiraud's—two six-man parties: one goes east, the other west | 55 miles |
| May 15 | Hears that the California Gulch boys had killed a Mexican, supposed to be one of the murderers, but his companion had escaped: the Espinosas | |
| July 14 | Puts on play at Buckskin Joe's | |
| July 17 | Fairplay to Bradford's | |
| July 18 | Bradford's to Denver | 90 miles total |
| July 31 | About forty men to go on detail | |
| Aug. 1 | Denver to the St. Vrain River | 55 miles |
| Aug. 2 | St. Vrain to Big Thompson | 8 miles |
| | Big Thompson to Cache la Poudre | 18 miles |
| | Cache la Poudre to Camp Collins | 14 miles |
| Aug. 3 | Camp Collins to the Boxelder | 16 miles |

| | | |
|---|---|---:|
| Aug. 4 | Boxelder northeast to old Fort Walbach (near Cheyenne Pass) | 45 miles |
| Aug. 5 | Fort Walbach north/northeast to the Chugwater | 50 miles |
| Aug. 6 | Follows the Chugwater | 45 miles |
| Aug. 7 | Chugwater northeast to Fort Laramie | 20 miles |
| Aug. 9 | Fort Laramie southwest to "Sabeel" (Sybil) Creek | 38 miles |
| Aug. 10 | Sybil Creek to mouth of Horse Creek (he thinks), then to Laramie River (west/southwest) | 40 miles |
| Aug. 11 | West to Fort Halleck | 52 miles |
| Aug. 12 | Crosses the Medicine Bow southwest to Cooper Creek | 55 miles |
| Aug. 14 | Southeast to the Little Laramie, then to the Big Laramie | 32 miles |
| Aug. 15 | South/southeast on the Cherokee Trail to Virginia Dale | 40 miles |
| Aug. 16 | To Camp Collins and Collona (La Porte) | 20 miles |
| Aug. 17 | By himself, visits friend, Jack Hayword, on the (Big?) Thompson | 23 miles |
| Aug. 18 | Comes down the creek to visit cousin Henry | 13 miles |
| Aug. 20 | South to Camp Weld (Denver) | 50 miles |
| Aug. 25 | Accompanies Major Fillmore south to Cobley's Ranch | 37 miles |
| Aug. 26 | South to Colorado City | 33 miles |
| Aug. 27 | South to Pueblo | 50 miles |
| Aug. 28 | No mention of where or what direction; presumably east toward Fort Lyon | 46 miles |
| Aug. 29 | On the Indian reservation to Bent's Old Fort | 25 miles |
| Aug. 30 | Fort Lyon | 58 miles |
| | | |
| Sept. 3 | East following the Arkansas River | 7 miles |
| Sept. 4 | East following the Arkansas River | 20 miles |
| Sept. 5 | East following the Arkansas River | 28 miles |
| Sept. 6 | East following the Arkansas River | 20 miles |
| Sept. 7 | East following the Arkansas River | 25 miles |
| Sept. 8 | East following the Arkansas River | 25 miles |
| Sept. 9 | East following the Arkansas River | 25 miles |
| Sept. 10–23 | In camp on the Arkansas | |
| Sept. 24 | West following the Arkansas River | 30 miles |
| Sept. 25 | West following the Arkansas River | 25 miles |
| Sept. 26 | West following the Arkansas River | 40 miles |
| Sept. 27 | West following the Arkansas River | 30 miles |
| Sept. 28 | West to Fort Lyon | 45 miles |

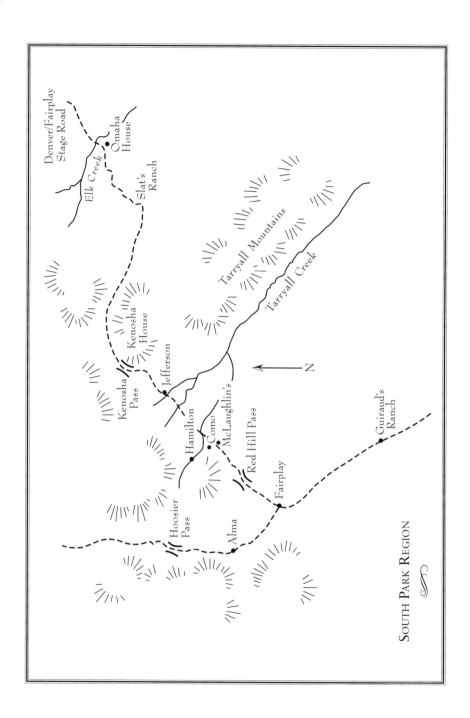

Denver/Fairplay Stage Road

Elk Creek

Omaha House

Slat's Ranch

Tarryall Mountains

Tarryall Creek

Kenosha House

Kenosha Pass

Jefferson

N

Hamilton

Como

McLaughlin's

Red Hill Pass

Fairplay

Guiraud's Ranch

Hoosier Pass

Alma

SOUTH PARK REGION

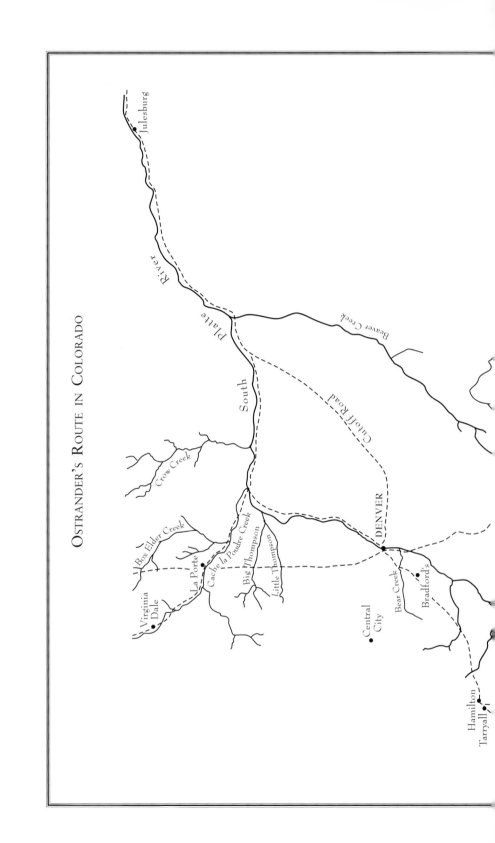

OSTRANDER'S ROUTE IN COLORADO

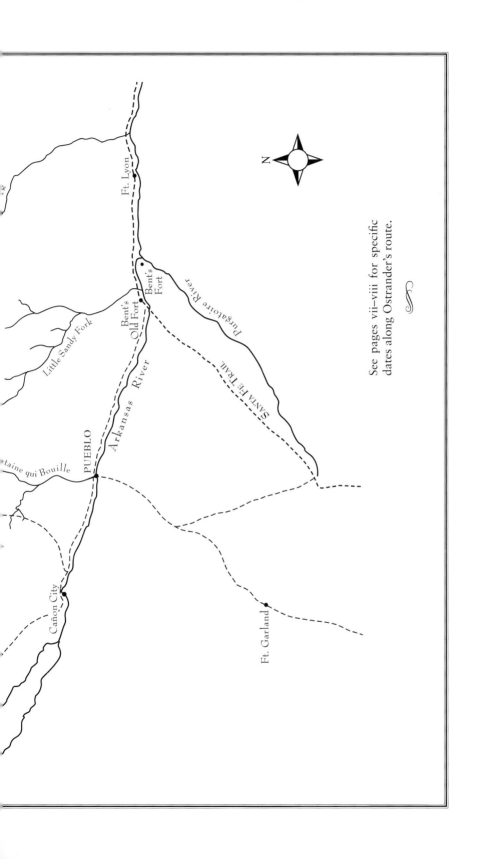

See pages vii–viii for specific dates along Ostrander's route.

## WYOMING

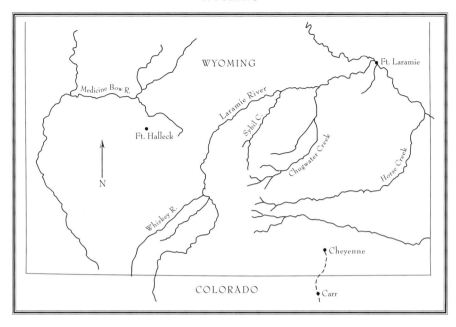

## NEW MEXICO

*T*his
*book is the*
*property*
*of*
*R. H. Ostrander*
*of Company F*
*1st Colorado Cavalry*
*A resident of*
*Roseville*
*Warren Co*
*Illinois*

One time when some of the boys were on picket near Pigeons rancho,[1] they were all sitting down in the woods near the road playing cards when one of them Bill Mencer[2] said he would ly down and try and sleep a little while. After he had gone to sleep they heard something on the road which sounded like twenty or thirty cavalry in full gallop; one of the boys ran upon a knoll to see what it was. Bill woke up with a start and being rather confused he lost his balance and rolled downhill and thirty yards crying out at every revolution "Where is my horse? where is my horse?" It was found to be a waggon.

I came very near shooting one of [my] comrads once (Geo Sowe).[3]

It was when our Company were going down to Santiago crossing. We had camped below Fort Lyon,[4] and by some means or other the Indians continued to steal a couple of our horses during the night. We remained in the same camp all day, and at night Lieutenant Nelson[5] divided the Co. into squads of five, and had them ranged around the camp about a hundred yards from it in a semicircle (the camp was by the side of Ft. Lyon). Our orders were to have one man on the watch in each squad at a time, who was to sit up in or near his bed and to shoot any thing that he saw moving without chalanging unless it was a man walking boldly upright.

It came my watch about the middle of the night and as I was not very well and had been on guard the night before I had not been up but a little while before I began to feel drowsy. I tryed with all my might to shake it off, but it grew upon me in spite of myself. I had no right to get up walk about or I should have done so. I would not close my eyse for a moment for fear of going to sleep but kept gazing about in every direction using every effort to keep awake, but after a while I found that if I let me eyes remain fixed upon one object for any length of time I was actually going to sleep with my eyes open.

I had roused myself out of one of these spells and on looking around I saw an Indian not over five paces from me sitting squatted on the ground and looking at me. As quick as thought I cocked my carbine[6] without noise (which can be done, be pressing the finger on the trigger, and to which I had practiced myself) and brought it to my face and was on the point of firing when I saw that it was George Sowe, who had (being probably impressed with the necessity of silence) noislessly crept out to attend to the wants of nature. When I saw who it was a shudder passed through me such as I had never experianced before. George went back to bed and as he never said any thing to me about it I conclude that he did not notice it.

After the above incident I was in no condition to stand guard. Every bunch of grease wood, or sagebrush, was an Indian. I could distinguis their voices as they conveyed signals amid the howling of wolves, which had had no efect upon me before. In fact I was under the influence of *fear—abject fear*—which (although I had been in three battles, and in places of danger where the bullets were flying thick around me) I had never felt before as I felt it now. After a little, although my time was not up, I woke the man who was to relieve me and crept to bed. but it was a long time before I could get to sleep, and when I did i started up every little while, as my imagination conjured up some horrable sight in my dreams.

The most disagreeable night I ever passed was the night of March 30th 1862. We had fallen back to San Jose[7] after the battles of Appache cannon[8] and Pigeons ranche, and there was a report brought in that there was a party of Texans in the neighborhood of Trickalo reet.[9] Ninty men, thirty of our Co., and thirty of each of two companies of Regulars, were detailed to go in search of them, under command of Captain Walker of U.S. 3d cavalry.[10]

We started about sundown in a northeast direction by a trail across the mountain guided by a Mexican. We got along very well untill after dark when it clouded up and was pitch dark. so we had to dismount and lead our horses in file along the trail, each man holding on to the tail of the horse before him. Up and down steep and rocky hills down and up steep and rocky ravines we went. I could not see the horse before me, and sometimes as those in advance would strike better ground they would walk out a little faster and we would loose them and had to stop and listen for the sound of their horses feet. Every few minits the words would come back along the line of "all up in the rear" and then back of "all's right." Thus we groped along for hours sometimes falling down among the rocks, sometimes running against trees, and sometimes crawling on our hands and knees. Once I slipped on a rock and fell either into a hole, or down the side of a steep bank. My horse heard me fall snorted and braced himself so that I saved myself by the bridle reins, by which I climed back. It had been raining a fine misty rain for some time and as we had got lost from the "advance" and could not trace the trail we concluded to stop. I saw what I took to be a tree a few rods off and started to hitch my horse to it, but before I got to it I was so exausted and sleepy that I sank down on the ground and was asleep. When daylight broke I woke up and looked for the tree. It was on the other side of a cannon and I had slept close to its brink. We found Capt. Walker with about thirty men and the guide not more than forty rods from us. They had passed the night the same as me, with their bridles in their hands. We proceded to Tuckalokeet and got there about nine o'clock p.m. but found no Texans, and no traces of any. The next day we met the command at Las Vegas.[11] By some mismanagement my blankets and clothing had been left behind and I never saw them again.

When the Colorado 1st left Denver to go into New Mexico, they were rather short of transportation and Colonal Slough[12] gave orders to press everything in the shape of it. This they did without respect for persons, or for the kind of transportation which happened to fall in their way. They took horses, ponies, mules, jackasses, and oxen promiscuously. The people on the Fountainquiboulle[13] and other creeks along the route were stripped of every thing that would serve the purpose, or that they did not run off and hide. They got the idea that we were stealing their property, forgetting that government does not steal and robb but while it sometimes impresses, it allways pays for property, however distant the payment may be. The news ran before us into Fort Union[14] that we were stealing all we could lay our hands on and robbing every boddy we meet. So that although the regulars received us with loud cheers and appeared glad to see us, they looked upon us as villains.

This oppinion was confirmed as far as our Co. was concerned the first night of our stay. We had made a forced march of ninty miles in two days and having eaten the last bit of grubb that morning were naturally rather hungry. Our officers marched us into a correll and left us to take care of ourselves, and went to look after their own comforts. Hungry men have few scruples, and as we found that if we did not look out for ourselves, noboddy would for us, we began to look about for something to eat. We had no money but going into the suttlers store[15] we saw some cheese boxes piled up. A couple of these soon found their way to the corelle, along with some square boxes, which looked like boxes of crackers but which proved to be champaigne. Somehow there was a box of crackers found its way to the correll finally, and we made out a supper, which if it wa'nt the best in the world, was *worth* about five hundred dollars cash. This as I said before confirmed the opinion of our lawlessness, and when we marched out of the Fort towards Santa Fe, a detatchment of regular Cavalry were sent two days in our advance, to warn the towns of our aproach. Every one of which was deserted when we passed through. And even after the fight great panes were taken to keep us out of the towns. We were allways marched as far from the larger ones as possable, while the regulars were marched through them to take possesion. This exasperated us, as we were confident we had done better fighting than the regulars, and for revenge we stole all the more when we got a chance, which didn't help the matter any however, and we were always used while in the territory like a set of half outlaws, which were tolerated but not to be encouraged on any account.

### February 26, 1863

I bought this book today and I am going to try and keep a diary. I have bought books before for the same purposes and I kept a diary once for about three months but that is about all the good it did me. I am going to see if I can't *keep* this one so here goes for a beginning.

I left Camp Weld[16] today with Cousin Henry who has been with me for three days and came to Golden Gate[17] on horseback fiften miles.

I have been lying about camp so long that it is something of a treat to get out for a little while. We came back from Golden Gate today. We had calculated to go up to Thompson Creek together but as he made a bargain with a doctor uptown to cure his leg for his pony we did not go any farther than the Gate. Henry has ben troubled with his leg ever since he and Fred and I were hunting togather but I hope that he will get it cured now for he is unable to work as it is.

It is reported in camp that we are ordered to the states but I don't believe it. Though I hope it is true.

### February 28

Well here I am in camp liveing the dullest kind of a life and likely to stay here for a while at least. We had inspection and muster to day mounted which got a little ahead of any other muster that I remember of witnessing for some time back. Cap. Cook[18] was out of humor and gave his orders all wrong and neglected to present sabers when he should have done so which made us appear awkward.

It has been a clear day but rather windy and cool.

### Sunday March 1

Last night I stood guard in the correll. I was detailed to go in the place of Mr. Shearer,[19] who was taken sick. 8 o'clock

Here it is the first day of March 1863 and I have been away from home nearly three years and to what purpose? Nothing! Oh how I should like to be at home for a little while if only for a little while to see how things look there.

There was nothing verry particular transpired in camp today. The boys are grumbling because there is nothing to eat. That is all.

### March 2

I went down town to see Henry last night and I had quite a visit with Dr. Huchinson and his wife and Hen. They are from Springfield Pennsylvania and are acquainted with a great many of my old acquaintants in West Springfield.

I have been on fatigue today and as it was the day to draw rations I have had pleanty to do. It is said that George C. Cook has been caut and came into town today.

What a dull life this camp life is.

### March 3

About two inches of snow fell last night which looked quite wintry this morning but it is all gone now. It seems curious that there is no more snow than there is in this country. The weather is much milder here than it is in the same latitude east and there is not near as much snow here as there is either on the planes or in the mountains. There seems to be a strip of country along the foot of the mountains here and about denver in particular that is skipped over by all the storms or only touched by them lightly. What is the reason of this?

### March 4

I went up town to day to get my boots mended and seeing Henry on the street stayed and chatted with him till after noon and so missed being sent out on detail as I found when I got back that Capt. Cook had gone with twenty men to Golden Citty, but for what purpose is no known. I should like to have went with this detail just for the sake of having something to do if for nothing else. and I should probably have went had I been here.

### March 5

Captain Cook and the boys came back last night after dark. They had been in search of Government property supposed to have been secreted in the house of a Mr. Pollard. They found nothing but after they had got back he found out that there was a trap door in the floor that he had not opened so there was another detail sent—of which I was one—to search further. We started at ten o'clock and it being a bright moonlight night we had a pleasant time but found nothing but brandy coctails and whiskey upon which the boys got rather salubrious.

### March 6

I had not room to say yesterday that the Third started for the states in the afternoon and were escorted through town by the First. There were speeches made by the Gov. and Gen. I suppose for we (Co. F) couldn't hear a word the wind blew so. We moved to day into quarters which were evacuated yesterday by a part of the Third. There was a funeral to day here to day of a Seargeant of Company A (George Gardner)[20] and Co. F furnished the firing party of fourteen and I was one of them. Every thing went off first-rate for a wonder if I am allowed the impression.

### March 7

I was put on guard last night at the Company Commisary and was concequently on guard to day till night. It comenced snowing about noon and still continues but it melts nearly as fast as it comes.

### Sunday March 8

Was on fatigue to day and had to carry watter for the cooks.

I received a letter from Annie this evening. There is a report in camp that the First are to be dismounted an that the Second are to have their horses which i don't believe.

### March 9

Henry came up to camp to day to see me but he did not stay but a little while. He said that he had to go back to take some medicin. He does not appear as cheerefull as I should like to have him. He is not talkative I cannot account for his reserve.

I received a letter from John Gardner to day. He and Mart have got through to the river all right.

### March 10

Nothing particular transpired to day except that the boys did not fall out to drill this morning untill the Captain threatened to put them in the Guard-house and then not all of them

Received a letter from Aunt Elisa this evening enclosed in one from Albert.

### March 11

Well it has been a pleasant day but as dull as ever. This life is the dullest life that I ever led and I believe it is as dull as any life that a man can lead.

Monotony! Monotony! Monotony! Every day just like the one that preceeds it.

### March 12

I don't know but it would be just as well to write D. for ditto along in here for there is nothing transpires in camp worthy of note. Nobody gets killed or wounded or hurt and I have nothing to do but to go on guard every fourth day and on fatigue as often. We had dress parade tonight and there was an order read about the trial and conviction of a member of some New York regiment who was sentenced to be shot. Also a letter about the instruments for the band. They are on the road.

### March 13

I have been at work pretty hard this afternoon and it has done me good. I think although I did not like to work at all for I am naturaly a little (I won't own that I am lazy) tired, and this soldier life does not help the matter any. I sometimes think that a man that soldiers two or three years will never be good for any thing else and I believe it is so in some cases. I wonder if *I* shall be fit for a citizen after my time is out.

### March 14

I smugled my horse out at watter call this morning and rode him up town. I saw Henry up there and had a long talk with him. There was a horse race at two o'clock so I stayed and went to it. It is the first time that my horse has had any exercise for several days and it did him good.

I mean to take him out oftener hereafter if I can for it did me as much good as him.

### Sunday March 15

We had inspection to day and dress parade this evening. I went to church this evening for the first time in a year and a half. I wrote a letter to Aunt Elisa and one to John Gardner to day. The orders read on dress parade were that no trooper should ride his horse except he had a pass or was going on drill. The same order was read some time ago but there has been more rideing horses without passes than with. I wonder if it will work this time.

### March 16

The ride I took day before yesterday did not do me so much good after all, for I caut cold and it's settled in my thies making me so stiff I can hardly move. Jessie[21] wanted me to go on fatigue to day but I told him I was not able to work; he said I would have to work or go to the guardhouse. I told him to the guardhouse it is then, for I am not able to work. I did not work and I have not been put in the guardhouse yet, but I don't know how soon I shall be.

### March 17

I don't know what to write in my little book to day. It is so hard to write when there is nothing to write about. I hadn't been put in the guardhouse as I expected.

I made a bet to day of fifty cents with Blakey.[22] that I would have ten dollars one month from today.

### March 18

We were paid off to day up to the twenty-eighth of February and the boys are feeling pretty jovial over it.[23] Some of them have got pretty salubrious as usual. After I was paid off I went to find Henry. Mrs. Huchinson said he was not there so I hunted about town for him but came home without seeing him.

### March 19

It has been rather windy to day but not verry cold. It was so dusty that it was disagreeable to be out. I have not been farther than the stables. My throat is a little soar and for that reason I don't like to go out much.

### March 20

On guard to day nothing in particular else.

Oh! for something to do! I wish the order would come for us to march to the states immediately. Here I have given three years of my life to Uncle Sam expecting that he would make use of it and he has made use of only about six months of it and the rest as far as I can guess is to go to waste, of no use to me nor to him. Oh! for something to do! Oh! for the road again!

### March 21

Killmore and Jake Bales[24] made a race on Killmore's horse against one in Co. C which came off to day at eleven o'clock. They had bet about one hundred and fifty or two hundred and offered to bet more on the ground but were not taken up. Our boys had pleanty of money there and would have bet five hundred if they could but no boddy would take it, which was lucky as it turned out, for Killmores horse was beat by a foot and a half.

### Sunday March 22

This is the anaversary of the day that we left Fort Union to meet the Texan army at Appache cannon. We burried one of our comrads, Addam Prichard,[25] to day. He died verry suddenly. He was not sick but three days. I don't know what ailed him and I don't believe the doctors do either. Though they say it was congestion of the lungs brought on by hard drinking.

### March 23

There was about four inches of snow on the ground this morning, and I had some fine sport snowballing but it is most all gone now. The sun has been shining all day, it looks like spring. Henry came to camp to see me this afternoon and Mr. Gaffney called in just at night a little while. His son Randolph has gone to the river to bring his daughter out here.

I am going down town with Henry this evening.

### March 24

I went down town with Henry last night and we went to meeting togather.

The ground is still wet from the recent snow, some of which still remains in shaded places. The mountains are a varigated mixture of white and black and gray as the gray hills the pine forests and the snowcapped mountains revele themselves in the bright sunlight. Company C started for Ft. Garland[26] to day.

### March 25

The snow has all gone now except on the mountains and there is verry little to be seene there except on the snowy range. Company M started for the Cachelapoudre[27] to day, where they are to be stationed, and we were all mounted and escorted them through town on their road. Why we did not escort out Co. C yesterday is more than I can tell. They are the only troops that have left here without the whole command falling out.

### March 26

This is the aniversary of the Battle of Apache cannon and the Captain had the company fall into line and fire five volleys in honor of the day which was done admirably. I don't believe it can be beat by any company in the army. I am on guard again today.

Dress parade again to night. The adjutint[28] is reading a great lot of orders I suppose but as I am on post and a good distance from him I cannot hear them. Our officers treated the company to three kegs of lager beer and they brought a quart, all drank the toast of: To the memry of our comrads who fell in Apache cannon, may they never be forgotton.

### March 27

Was on post this morning from five till nine and consequently was not here at breakfast. Cooks said there was nothing cooked so I had to wait till dinner.

The four twelve-pound howatzers have been manned to day, and they have been drilling in loading for the purpose of fireing a salute tomorrow. Oh dear I wish we were on the road again, going anywhere, to do anything. I would rather be in the saddle evry day than to be lying around this way. I am heavily sick of it.

### March 28

I was awakened this morning by the sound of the cannon at sunrise. A salute of thirty-four gunns were fired in honor of the day, it being this day one year ago that we fought the battle of Pigeons Ranches. At eleven we were all mounted and fell into line on the parade ground. From there we marched down town and all around town with banners flying and making a big splurge generally, after which we listened to flattering and patriotic speeches from Gov'n'r Evins, Sec'y Walbod, At'y Gen'l Brown, Colonel Chivington, and others.[29]

At sundown another salute was fired. The boys handled the guns first-rate, notwithstanding they are green hands.

*Sunday March 29*

I went to the Presbyterian church this forenoon, I liked the sermon pretty well. He is a young preacher, but he is well educated and eloquent.

This afternoon I went down town and went to the methodest church with Hen. this evening.

*March 30*

We went out on drill this forenoon and had some fun in the shape of target practice with pistols on horseback in full gallop.

It has been rather windy this afternoon and the dust flew so as to make it disagreeable being out. Consequently I staid in the quarters.

*March 31*

After watter call this morning I went down town and Hen. and I went to the picture gallery and had our pictures taken for photographs. After that we went out and loafed around town, till towards night when I started for camp. In passing the commissary I overheard a waggonmaster talking to Lieutennant Anderson[30] about hiring a couple of teamsters so I went back and hunted up Hen. took him to the waggonmaster and he hired to him.

*April 1, 1863*

I am on guard to day and to night I stole my horse out at watter call and went down town and got those photographs and stopped a little while at Mister Gaffney's shops and had quite a talk with him on the subject of religion. He thinks that I ought to come to the methodist protracted meeting and get religion. After that I went and took leave of Henry. He has hired as a Gov'n't teamster and started for Canon City[31] to day.

*April 2*

I came off guard this morning and have spent most of the day getting ready to go to a dance on bear creek. Charley Wendell[32] and I are going to hitch our horses togather to a light waggon. John Ferris[33] introduced me to Mrs. Havens who is my partner. Her husband is a member of the second regiment.

*April 3*

I have just been woke up out of a nice sleep to go after some watter. I went to a dance on bear creek last night. We had a nice time and came home after daylight this morning. I have slept most of the time today.

*April 4*

Have had nothing to do today except to ly around camp. (Indeed, I might write the same nearly evry day and not be far from the truth.)

*Sunday April 5*

Have been down town to day, went to the brewry and drank some bere and got pretty near tight.

I am dilated to go somewhere with a lieutennant of Company R. We are to take fifteen days' rations.[34]

Volunteers were called for and I volunteered to go. Anything but camp life for me.

*April 6*

We got started this morning. General Chivington[35] is with us. I went down town before I started and sent off those photographs. We came to Cobely's Ranche thirsty seven miles to-day. The Lietennant says that the General is going down the country to look after those gurillies and that we may have some fun before we get back. I hope we will.

*April 7*

We left Cobely's this morning and came to Colorado City[36] thirty-three miles. This traveling after an ambulance is pretty fast business, for these officers like fast driving and have no marcy on animals.

Four or five of the boys brought their dinner and the rest had to wait till the waggon got up, which was about sundown. Half officers were with the ambulance and the ballance with the wagons.

*April 8*

We came from Colorado fifty miles to the Callifornia ranche on Cherry creek to-day. Seven of us travailed with the Officers and the ballance with the waggons which have not got in yet and probably will not till after midnight.

We should have been a tight row of stumps for grubb had not Colonal Ford[37] ordered supper for us. There is nothing for our horses but hay.

I am on guard to night.

*April 9*

The ambulance went on into denver this morning and we came in at our leasure. It is thirty miles. Our horses had about half a feed of corn this morning. They are pretty well fagd out with the last three days' travaile.

This rushing around the country after gurillies with an ambulance and not finding any is played out with me. The next time any of these Officers have a trip of that kind on hand they can get somebody else besides me to go with them if they please. I shall not volunteere anyway.

### April 10

Have been lying in the quarters to day. It commenced raining this morning a fine drizling rain which worked itself into a light wet snow before noon and continued till about four o'clock, making it rather disagreeable being out. All but one of our detail got in about one o'clock to day. Tommy Allen[38] has not been seen since we left Colorado. He stopped behind to get his boots mended and it is feared that he is lost on the Arkansas divide. I got a letter from mother to night.

### April 11

I stole my horse out of the corelle this morning at watter-call to exircise him and rode him uptown with Blakey. I called on Mister Gaffney. The Old man was glad to see me. It seems to do him good to have me come and see him. He is a fine old gentleman and I like him better the more I am acquainted with him. He thinks I ought to get religion.

I got three letters for Henry to day, one from Billy, one from his mother and one from mountain City[39] that I did not open. Tommy got in last night.

### Sunday April 12

I have just finished reading a volume of poems written by T. Y. G. Stocton which was loaned to me by Mr. Gaffney. I like it pretty well. I am on guard again today. One of Company L came here last night and has been here all day. He says they have killed one of those guerillas and captured two more. He was one of the party that captured them. Company K got in to day they have been down on the divide looking after the guerillias.

### April 13

The boys keep asking me if I am going to fight Foley.[40]

He and I had a part of a fight, the other day, about nothing, which was very foolish in us both and which I did not cronicle; and he has been bragging to the boys that he can whip me; and that he will fight me for fifty dollars; and as I don't think he can, I shall take him up if he chalanges me. I do not want the name of a prise fighter, but the temptation is considerable for fifty dollars.

*April 14*

Have been on watter fatigue today. There was another detale of twenty men called for out of this company today so I volunteered again. We are to take twenty days rations this time. I wonder if we will be more than four days gone! I hope so any way. I went down town and got my horse shod and took that book to Mr. Gaffney this afternoon.

*April 15*

We got started about nine o'clock this morning. First we went down town and then went out on the road towards bear creek to the bridge across the platte and waited for our commanders who are Lie't's Wilson and Oster.[41] From there we took the bearcrek road to the Pennsylvania ranche and from there to Bradford, where we are camped. It is about fifteen miles[42] from denver. There are twenty of Co. E with us. We left our sabers at home this time.

*April 16*

We left Bradford this morning and took the Tarryall road[43] first—up Bradford hill into the mountains which is about three miles long and winds and zigzags in every direction. (That is the road.) After which we have come down gulches up ravines and through pine timber all day. At last we came down about two miles to the platt and camped. We traveled about thirty miles.

> Oh! a life in the mountains,
> Where the scene ever changes
> As you traverse the ranges
> And breathe the pure air
> So wholesome and rare
> And drink from pure fountains
>
> So much better than stopping
> In city or town
> Where people throng
> With their stacks and wares
> Their fabrics and shares
> Their railroading, trading and shopping!

Our horses had no grain last night, and there is but fifty lbs tonight for forty horses.

### April 17

We broke camp about an hour after sunrise, and travailed up the creek; the north branch of the south platt, for about ten miles crossing it fifteen times. It is about as large here as south clear creek, with bright mountains covered with spires raising abruptly on either side. We took the south fork of it and the south fork of *that*—until it dwindled to a mere rill of pure spring watter. We have camped at the Kenosha house.[44] It is twenty miles. It has been rather cool today and has tried to snow a little but did not make it out yet. There are patches of snow lying around over the hills in shaded places. No corse tonight.

### April 18

After travailing about five miles this morning we came down a big hill into the south park.[45] It does not look as I expected it would. It is a kind of a bason of prarie surrounded by high mountains on three sides and covered with hills in the southern part of it. It is about 80 miles long, reaching to the Arkansas, and twenty or thirty miles wide. The hills are capped with pine and look black in the distance and they are all over it except the northern end. We left Taryall about three miles to our right and came into Fairplay[46] twenty five miles. It is a very small town of log houses and dirt roofs. It has been pretty windy to day and quite cold.

### Sunday April 19

Ten of our Company and ten of E Company were detaled to go out with five days rations on our horses. An old man by the name of Hawkins who had a pony stole two nights ago went with us as guide. We went fifteen miles on the Canon City road where we struck a trail which was supposed from known facts to be the trale of some of the guerillas, which we followed up into the mountains in a western direction. We found one horses and two ponies but no guerillas. We followed the trail till sundown and camped in the *[last two words unintelligible]*.

### April 20

We remained in camp, which was at buffalo springs,[47] untill about noon and had some fine sport shooting trout. We passed the salt works five miles after leaving camp, and then took a southwestern direction, to the head of trout creek, which is a large spring, issuing out of the ground at the foot of a large precipitous rock, making a creek large enough to run a big grist mill. We have camped about one and a half miles from the head. I picked up a tin plate at the saltworks, which we used for a frying pan to cook our trout. Have travailed 15 miles.

### April 21

I slept rather late this morning and consequently was behind getting started. The boys left the pack animals for Strupe[48] and me to drive and we had an awful time of it for the packs kept coming off and we travailed like h—l. We went down trout creek to the Arkansas river[49] and down it to Brownville and as we could find out nothing about the payhamkers we came back on to trout creek and camped for the night having travailed thirty five miles to day. We killed some rabbits this afternoon which we eat for supper. I saw deer sign in the neighborhood of camp.

### April 22

I got permission for Tantum[50] and myself to go on ahead and hunt this morning. So we took to the mountains, and travailed around over some pretty rough country trill about noon and as we found nothing, and but little sign, we went down in to the park and travailed on into camp. When we were about four miles from Weston's we saw four mounted men comeing toward us which we took for gurillas but they proved to be soldiers from Fairplay. They took us for guerillas and came to take us. We went to weston's ranch and found the command there, where we took supper and then came on to Fairplay. Jessie took two men to day who are suspected. 58 miles to day.

### April 23

There has been considerable excitement here about the two prisoners the boys took yesterday. Carle Man and Dutch Mike. They would like to get hold of them and hang them. Carle Man was released this evening as it was asertained that there could be nothing proven against him.

I made a mistake about the park. It does *not* reach to the Arkansas river. It is a prarie country and surrounded by mountains on all sides. The north and west sides are high ranges of snow. The south side is low mountains covered with pines. The east is higher pine mountains with an occasional snowy peak.

### April 24

The park is about fifty miles long, from northeast to southwest, and forty the other way; and is interspersed with hills, or small mountains, capped with pines. The hills take up but a small part of its area however. It is at a very high altitude.

Ten men were sent out to day, with four days provisions, under Sgt Keel to look for the trail of two men who were seen in the neighborhood of Hawkins' house yesterday. Four men went with the Lieutennant to Buckskin Joe's.[51] There were ten men left the other day at Weston's with Lieutennant Oster, as there had been an ox killed in the neighborhood.

### April 25

Lieutennant Oster came in to day from Westons leaving three men there. Lieu't Wilson also came back. A man came running into town, this evening about dark, and said that he had been shot at, and chassed by two men, three miles from here towards Buckskin Joe's. He said that he saw a man that lives in this town by the house of McCarter a little while before and he thought that he was killed. A half dozzen men and some cittizens went to look for him and found him shot in the breast and cut in the forehead with the but of a gun or some sharp instrument. He has a brother living here.

### Sunday April 26

Some cittizen thought he heard a couple of gunshots in a northeast direction about seven o'clock last night and it was thought that the murderers had possably gone over into veever gulch, and killed somebody. So Lieuten't Oster, and five of us went over to see about it. Nobody had been killed and there had no gunshots been heard in the neighborhood. Ten of us with Lieu't Wilson, and about a dozzen cittizens went to look for the trail to day. We found it, and followed it, till about the middle of the afternoon when we lost it. We hunted about three hours for it and then gave it up as a bad job and came home. The people are scared nearly to death here none but the bravest dare go out at all.

### April 27

One of the boys came rushing in about nine o'clock, and said, two more men killed Lieutenant, whereupon he jumped up from a game of poker and sung out *saddle up!* Which was done in about the time that it takes me to write it. Lieu't Oster with three of us sent down to Guirand's ranche[52] about

12 miles from Fairplay to keep watch from a hill, while Lieu't Wilson went to look for the corpses, and the trail. He found them at the red hills. One shot through the heart, lying in the road, and the other a little to one side, shot in the arm, and cut in the head with a hatchet. He found the trail of but one man, and he had macisins on, as every trail we have followed has been, which he followed till dark and then came in here about 8 o'clock.

### April 28

We left Guirand's about sunrise dividing into two parties of six each. I went with Mr. Hawkins[53] over to the east side of the divide while the other party kept the west side. It was the caculation to go arround the mountain and look for the trail of the fellow that was lost last night, and as it had snowed last night about two inches we thought we could find it if he had moved. We did not find his trail but we found a loose poney, and came across some cittizens of Fairplay, who said the trail we were hunting was that of a man who saw the boys yesterday and took them for guerillas and ran all day and came in after dark. He was scared nearly to death and threw away his coat hat comfiter and handkerchief. 55 miles to day.

### April 29

All quiet to-day, three men have gone to the Kenosha house with six days rations, three to McLaughlins Ranche,[54] and three to Buckskin. Some of the cittizens think they have found the trail of the horses of the murdered men. The murdered men were burried today. They are from California Gulch[55] and their names are Leland who was a store keeper, and Vinton.

Our horses are getting pretty nearly used up with this hard travailing, they do not get grain more than one third of the time. We have heard that our company have gone to Fort Lyon.

### April 30

Strope came in from Weltons to day and said he had found some fresh mocasin tracks and wanted some of the boys to go with him on the trail. Four men were sent with him, and eight went down to Guirand's with Oster. Five or six cittizens went on the ponies trail this morning. They wanted some of our horses for packing. Would not have the ponies, said they wanted good horses or none. Had not sence enough to know that the ponies were the best. Thought things were at a pretty pass when government horses could not be had for such a purpose.

*May 1*

I went with one of E Company this afternoon to escort the stage to Buckskin. It was escorted by some of our boys from the Kenosha house here. The people have comenced mining here a little. The most of the ranches in the neighborhood are deserted, the people having moved into town.

*May 2*

We came back from Buckskin this morning and the mail carrier on the Callafornia Gulch rout came with us and two of the boys went with him from here. Two men were taken prisoners by the boys at McLaughlins, and brought in here to day but they were released an hour afterwards. All of the boys that were out on trail have come in. They found nothing. All quiet here. The weather is fine. It looks a little like a storm.

*Sunday May 3*

A detail of eight of us under Lieu't Oster took four days rations, went out on the road towards Denver to be stationed along the road as escorts for the coach. When we were just this side of Snider's with a prisoner by the name of Baxter, who they had taken this morning at Sniders. They went there last night to take them and were fired on from the house, having a mule killed. They watched the house till daylight and then arested them. I was ordered to go back with the to men and help to guard him.

*May 4*

We stopped at McLaughlin's last night and left there this morning at nine o'clock, when within a mile of Fairplay we met some of the cittizens to whom we dilivered the prissoner. He was known to be an outlaw having escaped mail in Dinver once and from the sherif once. They took him out in the timber and hung him to a tree. Oh it was a horrable sight to see the poor fellow hung and he all the time protesting his inocence even to the last breath. But I don't know but it was justice, for he was undoubtedly an outlaw and all outlaws are dangerous charecters now.

*May 5*

I have been doing nothing to day. Went up the creek a little way to look at the miners at work. They have just got watter here in a long ditch which they have been repairing. I don't think they will ever make much money here untill they consollidate and mine on a bigger scale.

The way they are working at pressent is by letting the watter run down the bank, which it washes away, and then through a sluice carying the dirt with it, while the men are at work picking out the boulders which compose four fifths of the ground.

### May 6

We are still living in Fairplay. That is part of us. The most of the boys are scattered at different ranches along the road from Buckskin to Slatts for the purpose of acting as escorts for the stagecoach once a week. The weather begins to look a little like spring. It is at least a month behind Denver in that respect. I seems that we are to stay here all summer or for a while yet any way, and I had much rather do it than go to Fort Lyon where the rest of the Company have gone.

### May 7

My horse has got quite lame. I had to by some Sulphur to cleanse his blood. I wish I had the power of language to express my thoughts on paper.

I rode old George out a little way to exersise him this afternoon, and one of the boys, Winches,[56] went with me. He rattled on all the time in a continual train of small talk about his horse and a thousand other things. I was in a reverie about I don't know what, and only replied to him in monasyllables, and I suppose he thought me a verry dull companion and mad about something, as the boys frequently say of me.

### May 8

I was sitting on the bank looking at the miners at work below me this afternoon. Of the thousand things that crossed my brain I have now only a faint remembrance. I thought of all the differant places I had worked in as a miner. Of the hardships I had endured as such, and of the hardships of a soldiers life, and if I remember aright I came to the conclusion that a soldiers life is much the easier—and attended with but little more danger, and were it not for the restraint on one's actions as a free American, full as pleasant.

### May 9

I have been playing a few games of billiards to day. I have often sat and watched others play before but this is my first tryal of my own powers. It is certainly a beautifull game but proves rather costly to me, as I find I can play just well enough to get beat. Billiards is litterly a game of science, combining all the properties of lines, angles, motions and force; and it requires considerable practice to be anything of a player. I think it is like mathamatics impossible to become perfect in.

### Sunday May 10

Played a few game of Billiards this forenoon and was detaled to go to denver this afternoon. Came as far as the Kenosha house and my horse being lame, I changed off with Blakey, who is to go on in the morning in my place. There seems to be nothing else to talk about now but murders and guerillas. People do not travail now except in parties of five or six and every boddy is well armed. I overtook a man on the road today who was just putting up his revolver; not being certain who I was till I came close to him.

### May 11

The boys went on to denver this morning, and I stayed here with Tantum and Allen. We are verry near the top of the divide between the valley and the park, and about five miles from the park. The Kenosha house is a story and a half high, and is built of hewn logs. It contains four rooms, the barroom dining room kitchen and upstairs, besides a small cabbin at one side and to the rear, which is used as a lumber room, and where we cook our meals. There is a big stable capable of holding thirty horses, with a loft which is our bedroom.

### May 12

Herriman[57] is the name of mine host of the Kenosha house, and a fine man he is too. He surely knows how to keep a hotel.

There are two little children here: a boy about eight (who has a mexican jinney and a little waggon, which he keeps at work all the time), and a little girl who is just old enough for a plaything, and is continually running about and climbing on to some of us.

This is much pleasenter than life in Camp Weld.

### May 13

I will try my hand at a word picture of the locality here. On the left of the house the road from the park comes down a hill out of thick timber and crosses a little rivulet of melted snow and passing between the house and a rockey point of about the same hight, it crosses a little stream of about four sluceheads a little to the right. In front (beyond the little rockey point) there is quite a little streatch of open ground through which runns the little stream beyond. There is pine timber farther on undulating hills clad with pines and in the distance some of the peaks of the snowy range.

### May 14

This morning we all saddled our horses, including Mr. Herriman, and went down to the platt about six miles to fish for trout. I lost my hook and line before we got there and the others did not find any fish. It was proposed that we should go farther down to the forks and try again. Accordingly we went down about four miles where after looking up and down the creek about an hour and finding no trout, and Tantum falling in, we gave it up and came home.

### May 15

The stage came along about eleven o'clock. We were saddled up and ready to go with it. It was full of passengers. We heard that the Callafornia gulch boys had killed a mexican supposed to be one of the murders.* He had a companion who has escaped. We came to the Talbut house kept by Mr. McLaughlin.

### May 16

Last night, or rather this morning about two o'clock, the boys came up from the Kenosha house with an express from Denver, which had to go through to Fairplay. Tantum and Rice[58] went through with it. It is the names and discription of six prissoners who have escaped from the jale in Denver. We

---

*The Mexicans Ostrander refers to are none other than the Espinosas. Brothers Filipe and Vivian Espinosa went on a killing spree throughout south-central Colorado in 1863. One of their victims, A. N. Shoup, was the brother of 1st Lt. George L. Shoup, of the Colorado 1st Cavalry, Company L., who was sent to Fairplay to investigate. George Shoup went on to become a colonel, and eventually governor of Idaho and a United States senator from that state. John McCannon led a posse of citizens who killed Vivian Espinosa in an ambush. Some months later, Filipe and his cousin Jose Vincente Espinosa returned to raiding. Mountain man Tom Tobin hunted them down and killed them in October 1863, thus ending the career of Colorado's earliest serial killers, who may have murdered thirty whites from motives—personal, religious, and perhaps cultural—that are still unclear. See Clark Secrest's "The Bloody Espinosas" in *Colorado Heritage*, Autumn 2000, for a more complete account of the killings. Ostrander never mentions them by name, thinking perhaps that Confederate guerillas were the perpetrators of the crimes in the Fairplay area.

have orders to arrest them if we see them. Lieutenant Wilson passed here to day on his way to Denver. Three of the boys are with him.

### Sunday May 17

I passed allmost a sleepless night. The dogs kept up a continual barking all night, and I had a kind of a vague undefined idea that somebody was arround who had no business there, and consequently could not sleep. I got up two or three times and looked arround, but saw nobody. We came through with the stage to the Kenosha house this afternoon. Blakey is here. He expects me to go back to Fairplay but I have no notion to change back.

### May 18

Blakey went back to Fairplay this morning.

I am lying in the woods—*pine* woods, not such woods as I used to pick up chestnutts in nor such as are around Uncle Jed's house, back woods, nor are they like the hemlock woods where I used to hunt the ducks and trapp the squirrell. Still for some reason I have been think of all these, and a great many more. My memory goes back to other days when I used to go wintergreening, and blackberring, and wallnutting, and chestnutting, and of a thousand other things of childhood. Allass those days can never be recalled except in memory, and he is to be pittied who would stiffle memory.

### May 19

Oh why don't I get some letters. It has been over two months since I received one, and I know they have been written and sent several of them.

Yestereday was the birthday of my sister Annie, and I lay awake last night till verry late thinking of her and Ben and Albert, and Mother. Three years! It has been three years, and twenty-two days since I saw them. I wonder how many years and months and days will roll arround before I shall be permitted to see them again, and when the time comes will they all be there? Perhaps that time never will come! God grant that it may come and that they may all be there.

### May 20

I have just come out to catch my horse, who is tied in front of me, and is pawing and jumping about impatient to go, while I am sitting under a pine tree writing. There are pine woods behind me; in front of me is a small strip of prarie about a mile long and eighty r'd's [rods] wide. Over head are clouds with now and then a patch of sky vissable through them. To the left the mountains rise and fall gracefully covered with pines, for about five miles where are a couple of bald hills. In front (beyond the open space) there is a ridge of burnt timber. On the right there are pine clad hills and bald mountains innumerable.

Allen went to Fairplay today.

### May 21

Tantum and I saddled our horses and went to hunt for Mr. Herriman's horses. We saw a lake on top of a hill to the north of here, about three miles. It is about a mile long and a quarter wide as clear as chrystal and without on outlett. There is pleanty of grass on its margin.

There were a few scurries of snow, and it was a little windy, making it rather cool riding. We stopped and let our horses pick a little while on some good grass on a sidehill. The grass is getting pretty good here in some places.

### May 22

The stagecoach came along about ten a.m. with which we came to the Talbut house.[59] We saw a small herd of antelope on the park near the road. They looked at us a moment and then galloped off out of sight.

We met Blakey here. He came over from Fairplay today to act as a witness in a lawsuit which Mr. McLaughlin is having in Hamilton[60] about a cow. Lieutennant Wilson has been down to denver and he passed us today on his way back.

### May 23

The weather has been verry fine today being quite warm and but few clouds. The snow has nearly all dissappeared from the mountains being vissable only on the highest peaks and in shaded places on the north side of the larger mountains. There is one of the small lakes so common in this country about a mile from and in view of the house. It is about 500 yards long and 300 wide. We were trying the range of our rifles at it the other day. We found they would carry to it with perfect ease.

### Sunday May 24

We saddled our horses and went on into Hamelton two miles where I bought a pair of mocasins and left my boots at the shop to be mended. We had to wait untill about noon for the stage to come along. There were three gentleman who rode along with us on ponies from Hamilton. We met Mr.

Herrimann on top of the hill three miles from here. He had rode out to meet us. It has been a fine warm day. Shearer came from Fairplay with the coach to take Allens place here.

### May 25

Tantum and Shearer went out hunting this morning while I stayed and washed some shirts. They got in about noon and said they had found a deer lick and seen eight deer. They made a screen of brush where they intend to hide and watch for deer. We went out about an hour before sundown and the boys remained by the lick to watch while I took a sircuit in the timber to see what I could find. We all got in about dark having none of us seen anything to shoot.

### May 26

The boys went out again this morning at daylight to their deer lick but came back again for breakfast without any game. After breakfast I took my rifle and went to see what I could find. I travailed a good ways, saw some beautifull mountain scenery, a good many deer tracks, a couple of elk tracks, and a bear track, but as I could not shoot the scenery, and did not think it worth while to shoot the tracks, I came in about 2 o'clock without any game. Do not consider my time entirely lost however. Found the boys had gone off with Mr. Herrimann to look for a man supposed to be killed about a month ago.

### May 27

Shearer and I went out north to hunt and to look for a small lake among the hills. We travailed untill we were tired, and not finding the lake we came back. We saw no game except a rabbit and a coupple of squirrels, which we shot and brought home.

### May 28

We went at work this morning to build a fishtrap. We worked on it nearly all day but I doubt if it will catch fish now. It looks as if it would succle cows, however.

We are having nice weather these days. The grass has grown finely. Every thing looks green and fresh. There are some flowers in bloom. Summer has come at last, but it is not warm enough to be oppressive.

This is a pleasant country for a summer residence sure.

*May 29*

The stage got along about noon and Shearer and Tantum went with it. I remained behind because my horse is lame. The boys from slaghts[61] are here tonight. There are four of them. They tell great stories of their hunting and fishing down on the platt. They killed a bear the other day. All Cochran[62] wants to know if we stable our fishtrap of nights or picket it out.

*May 30*

Three of the boys from Fairplay came here today. They had started to come and relieve the boys at Slaghts, but they rec'd orders after they got started to tell all of the boys on the road to come in and to come back themselves. The boys were paid off at Fairplay today.

Tantum and Shearer came back here today to get their blankets. The team also came along on its way to denver after some more rations for us.

*Sunday May 31*

There are nine of us here. The ballance have gone with the team to Denver.

The stage came along at twelve o'clock and the paymaster clerk who has been to Fairplay to pay us off was in it. He stopped long enough to pay off nine of us who are here. We did not start for Fairplay today on account of waiting for the paymaster. We have passed our time in shooting fish, sawing wood, cracking jokes, etc etc etc.

*June 1*

The boys left Fairplay this morning, leaving me here to take care of the rations and blankets untill the team came back from denver. There has been a good many travailers along today. The excitement about guerrillas has about abated.[63] It is my opinion that Lientenant Wilson was drunk when he ordered all of the boys in off the road, and I should not be surprised if he sent them back again.

*June 2*

Had a long argument last night with a southerner who is a union man but not a Lincoln man about the war.

My horse being out of sight this morning I went to hunt him. I followed his trail due south through thick timber about three miles and had made up my mind that some thief had rode him off, but he took a turn finaly and came back to the house about half an hour ahead of me. He was litterly covered with muscitoes, which accounts for his travailing so far.

### June 3

Went with a man who stopped here last night to hunt a trail at the lake supposed to lead to the head of Chicago Creek.[64] We did not find the trail and he took off across towards the road. We found a bear which I accomodated with an ounce of lead. He putt off in a run without thanking me and I followed on in his trail for an hour when the ground became so hard I could not follow it. I hunted about for him a couple of hours and then gave him up and came home.

### June 4

Babcock[65] and one of Company E came here last night on their way to Slaghts to stop there and act as an escort for the mail coach between here and there again. Wilson has got sober I guess and so countermanded the order which took the boys off the road.

Tantrum and Sam Johns[66] came here this evening to remain here and Jessie sent an order for me to come to Fairplay and help herd the horses.

### June 5

The stage got here about one o'clock and as Tantum is not verry well today I took his place on the escort. Every thing passed off as usual. Sam Johns did not want to cook our supper nor I either, so we played seven up for it and he beat me.

### June 6

The people are as kind here as usual and accommodate us in every way that they can. One of Mr. McLaughlins children is verry sick.

### Sunday June 7

We went back with the stage to the Kenosha house and found that the teams have got back as far as here on their way to Fairplay. Some of the boys are gambling as usual.

### June 8

Four of the boys sat up all night and played poker.[67] I came with the waggons to Fairplay. Some of the boys are at work mining, and some are drunk, and some are doing nothing, and some are gambling.

Wilson has gone with five or six of the boys over on cash creek[68] fishing.

*June 9*

I was detailed for cook as soon as I got in, and had to go to work this morning.

We are living on Bacon, bread, coffee, beans, and potatoes.

There are two of us cooking. My boss got drunk this afternoon and weighs a ton if his word is to be relied on.

Some of the boys are so interested in a game of poker that they cannot stop to eat or sleep.

*June 10*

My boss was done cooking last night and was relieved this morning. I and boss cook to day. My assistant got drunk as soon as he could so I had to do nearly all of the work alone.

*June 11*

I was done cooking last night. Another man was put on cook in my place. The men are detailed for only two days now.

Wilson and the boys that were with him came back from their fisshing scout today. They tell big fish storries which are rather incredable but of course true.

*June 12*

Jessie put me on heard today. He thinks that he has got me here now and so he is going to putt me through. I brought the heard in at two o'clock.

I played a few games of billiards again this evening and as good luck would have it I did not have to pay for any of them.

*June 13*

Have been loafing about town—if it may be called one—all day. Played a few more games of billiards and won them by a scratch. It is rather dull liveing here with nothing to do. If it were not for the game of billiards we would die of enui. I don't know what ails me but for the last year I have been impatiant of my inactivity. I think that I can stand it better now than six months ago. Probably the excitement of our campaign in mexico is the caus of my constant impatiense.

*Sunday June 14*

Nothing particular has transpired today except that the boys have put on their clean shirts and so forth. It is rather dull business this keeping a diary with nothing transpiring of an interesting nature to full up with. If I was a good compositionist I presume that I might fill this my little book with interesting matter but as I am not it will have to go as it is: and as it is to be read by none but myself, and perhaps not at all, it makes but little difference.

### June 15

About the middle of the forenoon an old man came in to the quarters and wanted some one to work for him. I told him I would work for him and went along with him to his mining claim.

The work goes pretty hard with me for I have done none for nearly two years now (it is just twenty-one months and twenty-two day exacly). It is pretty heavy work rolling boulders lifting and wheeling them.

### June 16

Was at work for Mr. True again today. Felt rather stiff this morning but got over it as I got warmed up.

### June 17

At work again but quit in the middle of the afternoon to rest as this boulder mining goes rather hard with me.

### June 18

Was at work again this morning and kept at it all day.
Mr. True is a good miner in my opinion.

### June 19

There was a meeting here last night of some of the union men for the formation of a lodge of the Union league.[69] I was initiated and became a member of the order. Worked all day wheeling boulders.

### June 20

Worked till the middle of the afternoon when we quit to get ready to go to Buckskin (All. Cochran and myself) to be at a meeting of the league. I think that every union man should belong to it for there are undoubtly a good many coperhedds in this Territory and all union men should be able to know each other when they meet.

### Sunday June 21

Got home rather late last night, and consequently did not get up very earley this morning and so lost my breakfast. It has been a wet nasty day and pretty cool making a coat comfortable. There was some hail and a little snow with the rain.

*June 22*

Old man True has hired some cittizens for permanent hands and so turned us off. Consequently I have nothing to do now unless I get another job.

*June 23*

Was at work this afternoon for Pratt and company.

*June 24*

Went to work for Prat and company this afternoon again. Got wet as a drowned rat.

*June 25*

Went to work on the red hill for two and a half $ a day this morning.

*June 26*

Mr. Thompson is a first rate boss and a jolly fellow.

*June 27*

We got receipts for the amount of work done for our pay. I got mine cashed in fifteen minits after I rec'd it.

*Sunday June 28*

Every thing goes on as usual in the quarters. I am detailed for cook tomorrow.

*June 29*

I hired winches to cook for me and with Cochran and stephens[70] intended to work one of Mr. Trues clames this week. But we did not find it in as good condition as we had expected and so concluded not to go to work on it.

*June 30*

Mr. Kirkpatrick[71] (our new recruit) is getting up a Theater for the night of the fourth of July. He wants me to take one of the parts which I have concluded to do.

*July 1*

Have been studying hard all day. We made some tickets for the Theater last night.

*July 2*

We had a rehersal this afternoon.

*July 3*

Came here to Buckskin this morning to fix up our stage. We intend to stay here till Sunday.

*July 4*

We have got every thing all right. Had two rehersals this afternoon.

*Sunday July 5*

The M.D.A. gave their first performance last night. Every thing went off tolerable well considering that all but one of the actors were amitures.

We got back to Fairplay about three in the afternoon all right side up with care.

*July 6*

Felt rather lonely to day for want of something to do.

*July 7*

The boys told me that Old Man True left word for me last night to come and work for him a couple of days. I have worked today which is one.

*July 8*

Worked for Mr. True to day. My fingers are nearly worne through with handleing boulders.

*July 9*

Kirkpatric wants us to learn a couple of pieces and play them a few times here and see if we can't pay our back expences at Buckskin which we are going to do as our expences here will be comparitively nothing. The heaviest expence there was board, which will be nothing here.

*July 10*

We have found a room which will do for our theater by building a stage which we can do with some old lumber we have picked up. We cleared the place out today and painted a little.

### July 11

We have built a stage today which will do very well by carpeting it with blankets. We have also painted some of our scenery, all of which we had intended should be the best, had it not been for an order we got today to march to Denver next Tuesday. When we heard it after working hard two days, we were on the point of tearing our work in piece but the citizens told us to fix it as well as we could and give them one performance any way.

### Sunday July 12

We went at work again this morning painting scenery and fixing up our stage. We intend to give a performance on tomorrow night. We have worked hard all day. The plays will be the Golden Farmer, and Love in a Cottage.

### July 13

Was at work early this morning and got every thing ready by noon, so we had all the afternoon for rehersals. Our stage looks verry well though part of the scenery is blankets.

We have formed the acquaintance of nearly every boddy in the country here and they don't seem to like the idea of our leaving. Shouldn't wonder if they give us a good house tonight—hope so!

### July 14

Our play went off first rate last night and all express themselves well satisfied. We took in $51.00 which will pay all of our back expences, and more too.

I went to a dance after the Theatre and did not go to bed at all. We got started about nine this morning all the stores in Fairplay treated till nearly all hands were drunk. The people seemed sorry to have us leave, and I am sure the boys were sorry to leave for we have been treated as gentleman here and behaved as such.

### July 15

And now we will have to come down to the regular business of soldier-ing again. The boys look rather down in the mouth this morning and a good many of them are verry dry, for the reason that they didn't drink enough yesterday I suppose.

We broke camp about eight at the Mishigan ranche and came to the platt today where we caught fish enough for our supper.

### July 16

I went down the creek with John Webber[72] this morning and fished till about noon when we came on into camp which is at the Omaha ranch.

I brought in fourteen fish in my saddlebags but threw away 8 of them, they being spoiled.

### July 17

We left camp this morning and came to Bradford. I never heard the boys express any regrets at leaving a place before, but now it is nothing but "I wish we had stayed two months longer, I wish they would order us back," etc.

We have been living in a cool pleasant climate all summer, and I expect the hot weather at denver will go hard with us for a while.

### July 18

We left Bradford at sunrise and arrived in denver about ten. The weather is verry warm here. I went and called on Mr. Gaffny this evening. His daughter has got here. She brought a miniture to me from mother. She does not look any older than she did when I saw her as I can see. There are but few troops here and they are all straglers or small detales of the various companies. There is no whole Co. but the battery.

From Fairplay to Denver, 90 miles

### Sunday July 19

Have lounged about the barracks all day. Our squadd with several others here have been formed into a temporary Co. under the command of lieutennant Oster. The regulations here are verry loose now quite a contrast to last spring in that respect.

I comensed boarding at Maddam Thurston's[73] yesterday. We have to give one dollar a week and our rations.

### July 20

There is considerable business going on in denver now. Money is pleanty and there are several substancial brick buildings going up in the burnt district. Every boddy seems to have pleanty to do except the soldiers. I wish we had some thing to do also.

*July 21*

It is pretty hard to have to write something every day whether one has anything else to do or not. It would seem that if one had nothing else to do he might easily find subject of thought to fill one of these small pages. I presume most people would but I cannot allways do it. Not that I do not think but it is hard for me to put my thoughts in writing. My thoughts or reveries are often of such a nature that I don't know myself what they are, and probably could not write them if I did.

*July 22*

The weather—in the language of the poet—still continues! and so do I. That is, I still continue to be, to exist—if existance can be called a reallity: and if it is a dream, I still continue to dream.

*July 23*

I have nothing to do! nowhere to go! I am not acquainted with any body in this town, notwithstanding I have been here so much except Old Mr. Gaffney. I went to his house last evening and spent a pleasant little hour in chatt.

I was on fatigue today and helped to fence in the spring and drain it.

*July 24*

The boys seem to be enjoying themselves verry well. They are gambling nearly all of the time, but generally on a small scale. They play poker and monte mostly but they play the other games some. My bunkey has been dealing monte on a small scale, and some of the boys have been paying freezeout poker[74] for shirts and pants.

*July 25*

This day has been like all the others this week. Warm dry with a little breese in the afternoon which often increases to a storm of dust. The evenings are cool and pleasant with a clear skye and bright moonlight. Just the evenings for a nice little scout if we were only in the states, on the borders to have some

*Sunday July 26*

I went to church today. I notice that the fair sex are getting more pleanty in denver. One meets them allmost as often as the other sex now. This makes the citty have a more cheerefull aspect.

When I first new the place it wore a grin which showed all kinds of horrable looking teeth. Now those teeth have been repaired or concealed and the grin has gradually softened down into a smile.

### July 27

I find my boarding place much more pleasant than living in the cookhouse and full as cheap. Were I boarding with the company I should probably spend at least a dollar a weak for milk and vegetables and then everything is so much nicer to eat off a clean tablecloth and clean white dishes. Besides we live a great deal better. We have butter green potatoes, beans, and peas, pies, cakes, etc. every day. I have to pay one dollar a week besides my rations.

### July 28

Jim Hall[75] came in from Fort Lyon to day. He says the boys are scattered about the country down there in three or four different squadds. They pattroll the roads in all directions and when in post do not have to tend any but their own company guard.

### July 29

I called on Mr. Gaffney again last evening. The old man allways seems glad to see me. Was on guard today there is but one prissoner in the guard-house now. Have just finished reading a novel written by Victor Hugo. It is an old french novel and is quite interesting and I believe it is a true picture of human life. Les Meiserables is its name.

It is rumored in camp that we are to go and escort the paymaster some-where in a day or too.

### July 30

Have been lying about the quarters today and I might write the same of every day. I believe I do write it pretty often for want of something better to write. The boys are still amusing themselves gambling as usual. My bunkey started with thirty-five cents for a bank and dealt monte till he had won four or five dollars, five cents at a time. He lost it all in the same way though, so it didn't do him any good except the amusement.

### July 31

Forty of us were detailed to go somewhere tomorrow, and there is quite a hubbub in camp about who is going and who ain't going. Some that are not going would like to go, and some that are going don't want to go, and some don't care whether they go or not. They are the only ones that are sattisfied.

We are to take fifteen days rations and it is supposed we are going to escort the paymaster up north.

*August 1*

We got saddled up about eight o'clock this morning and after standing around about two hours, as usual, fell in and marched up town. After standing around in the hot sun an hour and a half, which time some of the boys improved in getting sober, we got started. We travailed pretty fast for about three hours, and then came down to a walk. One of the Co. E boys lost his private horse on the road: died by hard riding. We are camped on the St. Vrain.[76] 55 miles

*Sunday August 2*

We left the Saint Vrain about eight, and travailed pretty fast to the big Thompson,[77] where we stopped and let our horses rest and feed a while as the next strip was 18 miles without watter. We saddled up about one and travailed at a moderate pace to the Cache la Poudre and stopped at camp collins.[78] Co. B are stationed here, and are to be paid off to night. This is where the cherokee trail enters the mountains. The weather has been cool and comfortable but rather dusty.

40 miles

*August 3*

We remained at camp Collins and cooked up some bread this forenoon. There is a nice swiming place in the cachelapoudre near the camp, which the boys kept going all the morning. I am on guard today and left camp with the waggons at one o'clock.

The command left afterwards and passed us about 8 miles from camp.

We are camped on the Boxelder.[79] It is about 4 feet wide here and shaded by a thick growth of willows. The country is dry praries with some grass and a little rolling table mountains to the left.

16 miles

*August 4*

We travailed in a northern by eastern direction this morning with table mountain on our left for about twelve miles when we entered a cannon and assended to the top of the table land which looked like an interminable tract of level prarie, but proved to be cut up by ravines, which made the road rather hilly. We stopped on crow creek and fed, having come thirty miles without watter, though we passed it in two places a little off the road. We then came on 15 miles to old Ft. Walbeck[80] where is a good spring. (45 miles)

### August 5

Ft. Walbeck is at the entrance of Cheyenne Pass. There is nothing left there but the chimnies and part of a corelle now. The spring forms the head of a nice little streame. We came north by east over a rolling prarie crossing several little streams, which came down from a range of hills on our left. There are table mountains on the right. We entered a cannon through the table mountains formed by the Chugwatter,[81] where we stopped till the waggons came up, and then came on down the stream. While we were stopped there came up a hale storm which was terrifick. It flooded the stream. (50 miles)

### August 6

We have followed the Chug down today. It is a sluggish stream. There is some good farming land on it if it were not for the want of watter the creek would not furnish more than enough to irrigate one good farm. But there is some good grass and watter enough for stock. There is pleanty of wood, mostly Boxelder. There are table mountains on either side, which grew smaller as we came down. We stopped at about thirty miles where we made a sein of two gunny sacks and caught a lott of small fish. When the waggons came up we came on 15 miles. There are two kinds of currents, and some chokecherries. We travailed east by north. 45 miles

### August 7

We left the Chug this morning to our left and came over a rolling country in a north east direction twenty miles to Fort Larimer.[82] It is on the north side of the river of the same name. There are about forty lodges of Indians camped here.

The boys borrowed a seine and caught about a barrel of fish this afternoon. There are two companies of Ohio cavalry stationed here. They put on nearly as much style as the regulars but they are more sociable.

### August 8

The boys went down to the platt 12 miles to catch some fish but didn't have verry good luck. Indians have been lounging about the post all day. They are tolerable well dressed. I have been in several of their lodges and they appear to have pleanty to eat, most of them.

### Sunday August 9

We got started for Fort Hallack[83] this morning, where the Major has to pay off some more troops. We came 18 miles up the Jasime river and stopped to rest and grase awhile. When we saddled up we left the river on our right and took a south west course over a smoothe hard road on a level prarie 20 miles where the road struck the Sabel [Sybil], a creek destitute of watter except in holes, but pretty well timbered with cottonwood and boxelder where we camped. Chokecherries are in abundance. Travailed SW 38

### August 10

We came up the Sabeel to the mouth of Horse creek.[84] Crossing that we left the creek and in four miles enterred a cannon of a small dry stream. We soon crossed a little divide and found ourselves in the cannon of a larger creek which I think is horse creek, where we grased till the waggons overtook us. When we came on through the cannon raising till going up a hill, we found ourselves on table lands. We came nearly west over high rolling prarie till going down a pitch we found ourselves on Larime river again. There is not a stick of timber in sight. (W.S.W. 40)

### August 11

We crossed the river and took a due west course over very pretty rolling prarie but dry as usual. I am on guard and had to travail with the waggons. We crossed several dry cricks, some of which had a little watter in holes. About three we overtook the command graising on bear creek (40 miles). There is a dispute among the boys whether this is the north park or Larime planes. There are mountain on all sides of us. We hitched up and followed the command on into Fort Hallack 12 miles. It is situated at the foot of a large mountain.

Nearly west 52 miles

### August 12

This post is garrisoned by a company of the Kansas 9th Cavalry. The waggons and part of the troops who were up here on an indian expedition came in here this afternoon on their way to denver. The larger part of the command took pack mules and followed the trail of the indians down the west side of the mountains. The last news of them, they were out of grub, and the most of their horses given out. These mountains to the southwest and west are the Medicine bow mountains, and the plane to the northeast is Larime planes, a continuation of north park.

### August 13

The Kansas boys have made a horse race with the co. M. boys against the Jim Crow pony for twenty-five dollars, but I did not stay to see it as my horse is lame I started on ahead

We crossed several running streams: among which is the Medicin bow and travailing over a rolling country with heavy mountains on our right, and small ones in the distance on our left, we camped on cooper creek thirty-five miles from Fort Hallack. This is the U. S. L route and there is a station her, and two between here and Hallack.

(South west 55 miles)

### August 14

We left camp about an hour after sunrise and travailed at a moderate pace in a south by east direction over a rolling dry country with a heavy rang of mountains on our right, the Medicin bow I suppose, and a light range in the distance on our left, which we are gradually nearing, 15 miles to the little Larime Crossing that we came over a smothe road sometimes on high prarie, 17 miles to the big Larime, where we are camped. There are some good bottoms on these streams which would make good farmes, and pleanty of watter for irrigation but little wood

(east of south 32 miles)

### August 15

We had a very good road for 15 miles to the first station which is on a small uncertain stream. We than began to have a rough mountainious road winding about in all directions between and over the hills. We passed another station 30 miles from camp (in varginia dale[85]) and 10 miles from that we found another, where we camped. Our camp is a poor one as there is no grass. We have been travailing on the old Cherokee trail ever since we struck these hills. This is nearly the southern extremity of the black hills. They are principally table mountains but occasionally run up into rocky peaks. They run in a north eastern direction, are sometimes sparsely covered with pines and sometimes bald

E.S.E. 40 miles

### August 16

We came about twenty miles to Camp Collins today. Major Filmore bought some green corn and beans for us here. There is an old settlement here on this creek, called Collona.[86] It used to be called La Porte. It used to be a kind of a stopping place for trappers and indian traders. Mexicans, French, Americans and half breeds

12 [miles]

### August 17

I got permission from the Lieutennant to stop on the Thompson and see some of my old acquaintances.

I left the command about Eleven Oclock and came up the creek five miles to Jack Hayword's place. I found him in the field at work. he was very glad to see me and gave me a righthearty welcome. Jack has fifteen acres of corn on the ground I helped him to break up. he says he has made pretty well in this country but wants to sell out and go back to the states

23 miles today

### August 18

I went with Jack up the creek to look at his cattle this morning. he has twenty two head and some very fine looking ones. After dinner I bid good bye to Jack and with many good wishes and an invitation to call again I took my leave. I came down the creek in search of Henry. I thought at one time I was not going to find him but finely succeeded about sundown. I found him living on the farm of a Mr Johnson who has gone to the states, leaving Henry to take care of his crop, for which he is to have one third

13 miles today

### August 19

Henry and I had a long talk about old times and when that gave out we wrote some letters. We went in swiming and after dinner we had another long talk full of reminicinaes of the past and projects for the future. We then went out and he shot a couple of ducks which we cooked for supper: after which we talked again till bed time: thus we filled up the day in pleasant talk, which is not much to tell about, but pleasant to think about and long to be remembered by one at least

### August 20

I bid Henry good bye and mounting my horse, became aware that I am still a soldier, and have more to do with the real than the ideal. As I rode over the hot dry praries with the Rocky mountains on my right, and the boundless planes on my left, I became oblivious to every thing and passed the day in reveries: the top or bottom of which I can not write down; neither can I recollect the one tenth part. When I got to rock creek I unsaddled my horse and let him rest awhile, while I eat a lunch I had brought along: I then came into camp. I found the boys in tents

50 miles today

### August 21

There is quite a row in camp, about a beef the boys killed the other night. Killmore clames it also: and a cittizen clames it also: Killmore has been trying to find out who had a hand in killing it, but does not succeed verry well, allthough it is well known by all of the boys who did it.

We are camped at the south west corner of camp weld. The dirtiest corner of the place as a matter of course [is] some hospital tents. I went this morning with some of the other boys, over to Mrs. Thurstons to board because the cooking arrangements here in camp are not carried on in the *nicest* style immaginable

### August 22

Went and made a call on Mr. Gaffny's folks last evening and spent a pleasant hour. have been lounging about camp talking about the war, the new mines, the old mines, politics, reading the papers, playing cards, and blowing off our extry gass generally, as usual. The boys are verry indignant at Killmore about the beef question: they say he has allways been the biggest thief in the Co. and he aught not to try to expose them in the way he has. They swear they will retalliate by exposing some of his rascallities if he dont dry up

### August 23

Went to church this forenoon. Took dinner at Mr Gaffnie's as per invitation. and then to the sunday school this afternoon. I found it a verry interesting school, something like the one I attended eight or ten years ago, only the songs were mostly union songs. Full as pretty ones as the old ones.

It has been a pleasant day and quite cool: much more so than for a few days past. All of Co.s F and G are ordered to report to Lieutenant Oster tomorrow morning to go in escort of Major Filimore south we are to stay with our Co.s

### August 24

For some reason we did not start this morning, but are to start tomorrow morning. It seemes like pulling hair to some of the boys who have been here nearly all summer to have to go away just as they are beginning to get acquainted in denver society

I saw Justin Chritendn[87] to day and had a pleasant chat with him about old times in Conneaut Ohio

Our old acquaintances are scattered all over the united states. A great many of them are in the army now

### August 25

The waggons with the grubb blankets and forage started tolerable early this morning with orders to go on to Cobelies. I had to stay behind with the escort. We were ordered to be at the office at nine, which we did. We waited around in the sun for the Major to get ready from nine till two when we got started. Most of our officers are more like boys than men: this is not the first time we have had to saddle up and wait on them for hours, on starting out on a trip. We travailed very fast and reached Cobelies about eight Oclock

37 miles

### August 26

I had to travail with the escort again today although my horse is a little lame. We reached Colorado City about two Oclock and the waggons about four. I am detailed on bread cook to night

Colorado City looks as if it was deserted. (but one). The last time I was here it was full of soldiers of our regiment: some of them in the houses but the most of them in tents. Now there are but three or four families in the place and it looks dessolate

33 miles

*August 27*

It was said in camp this morning, that we were to go to Pueblo to today, so one waggon was left behind, as the boys were not willing to have their hosses driven in the team so far, and the mules were two of them dead, (they died day before yesterday) and the other givess out. Part of Co E was left with it, to reach Pueblo the best way they could in two days. We came on and stopped for noon a little below Youngs ranch some of the boys found a wattermellon patch of which I got a good feast. We came on and camped on the south side of the Arkansas below Fountain and above Pueblo

50 miles

*August 28*

Ten of Co. L, which is stationed her, were detailed to go with us and escort the Paymaster back from Fort Lyon.

Those who had lame horses were allowed to start ahead and travail by themselves this morning After we had come this side of Pueblo, about five miles I hunted along in the field for a mellon patch. When I had found one I signalled to some of the boys I saw stragling along the road, and eight of us made a meal off of four wattermellons. We nooned at Boosses ranche and then came on to spring bottom. The cropps I have seene today are better than any other river in the Territory

46 miles

*August 29*

We ar now travailing on the Indian reservation,[88] and there are no farms along here, as there was yesterday higher up the river. There are some good broad rich bottoms along here which would make a good many splendid farmes, and I have not a boubt but it will be settled before many years in spite of its being an Indian reservation.

We came to Bints old Fort[89] to day and camped for the night. I saw John McCormick[90] on the road yesterday he is stationed at Harrses ranche and has to forward the Government dispatches.

George Casidy is here for the same purpose. We met a war party of about twenty Arrappahoes today

25 miles

*August 30*

The Lieutennant told us he wanted us to get togather before we got to the post, so as not to go stragling in. We came on down the river and I crossed over to an island about fifteen miles from camp, and got some grapes to eat.

When about eight miles from here, four of us who were ahead, as we could see nothing of the command, unsaddled our horses and let them grase till the command came up. We found the boys were glad to see us and the usual shaking of hands, and "how are you old boy" had to be gone through with all around.

58 miles

### August 31

A good many of the boys are boarding out as some of us did in camp weld. Some of them are living in tents on the parade ground, on account of the bedbugs in the quarters. We made our bed in the open are [air] on the parade ground for the same reason. The boys that have private horses, had them prised today. The pay roll was made out and we signed it. Some of the boys got a little salubrious by some means or other.

This post is garrisoned by K Co. and F Co. of the First Col Cav, and two sections of the ninth Wisconsin Battery

### September 1

Well after an absence of four months and a half I suppose we will have to come down to the regular life of a soldier in camp again. I can see allready that it is going to be as dull as ever, allthough we have had pretty lively times here today. We were paid off this afternoon, and there has been the usual amount of inebriation and gambling, and an unusual number of fights. This evening there were three distinct fights and several quarrells. I thought at one time that all hands were going to pitch in for a free fight which came verry near being the case

### September 2

The game's "still go on" in the language of the sport. monte is the principal game, but the boys play a little poker 'tambian'. There have been several monte banks broken allready; but there is two or three which still hold out, though they also sometimes have heavy reverses: I guess however they make it win in the long run: at least aught to, for there is considerable percent in the favor of the dealer.

We got orders to be ready for a trip of a months duration in the morning:

so it is all up with me about boarding out as I had calculated. All are to go except the sick and a few for provosts.

### September 3

There is the usual hubbub of preperation for a scout this morning, but for all that there is but little cessation in the gambling: The Colorado First will gamble whether they do any thing else or not

We did not start as was expected, in the morning but got off about three in the afternoon. It is rumered that we are going down the river to settle with the indians for some depredation lately committed by theim on some of the trains.

There are twenty of Co. K as section of the battery and fifty of Co F. in all ninty four men with two pieces of cannon

7 miles

### September 4

Revillee sounded about daylight and we were in the saddle about half an hour after sunrise. We came down the river till about noon when we camped.

We saw old Bent[91] with his family and Indians, ponies etc camped by the river. He looks more like an indian than a white man, and lives more like one. He has lodges etc, but travails with waggons. He has quite a hird of ponies but there are verry few good ones and those he will not sell. We passed the camp of two stagecoaches and got some late news

20 miles

### September 5

We had a dozen indian warriers in camp last evening, all armed to the teeth with spears, bows and arrows, shields, revolvers, rifles. two of them came in soon after we had camped, and unsaddling their ponies stopped till near sundown, when the others came up. When they came to saddle up, one of them could not find his rifle, and he was greatly troubled about it. Our Officers tried to find it, but did not succeed. such is the example we set them

We started an hour by sun and camped about one Oclock

28 miles

### September 6

Well we have been travailing down the river again today. There is a good deel of good land along here, but it is all indian land I suppose. There is plenty of grass on the bottoms that would cut a good swathe and make good hay, but it is a good ways from market.

Indians are pretty pleanty we have seen several small parties on one side or the other of the river today. we camped under five or six cottenwood trees. This place has been used before and is called the pleasent encampment

20 miles

### September 7

We got our usual early start and came on down the river. Nothing of any particular interest transpired today. We camped on the river bank without shade. We used willows and buffalo chipps for fuel.

The boys still keep up their incescent gambling at every camp

The river is getting smaller or rather shallower, and more sandbarrs in it as we go down

25 miles

### September 8

We got started half an hour after sunrise and came down the river about twenty five miles.

It has been rather cloudy this forenoon and quite cool. The arkansas river is played out. there is nothing left but the sandy bed of the river and two or three little streams following it down which dissappear and show themselves again at intervals. The river, or the place for the river is about seventy rods wide, and it can be crossed like the red sea of old, dry shod.

The boys found some fish in a hole and as they do by every thing else that is lying loose, they gobbled them

(25 miles)

### September 9

We got another early start and came down the river. We met a train who said they had been robbed of part of their provissions by the indians. We wint into a camp of the Arrappahoes on the river about ten and stayed until about two. The indians were told that this robbing of trains must be stopped

They restored ten mules and a horse with the U. S. brand which we did not know they had

They said the robberies had been committed by Kiawas camped farther down the river

We came about ten miles farther down and camped

I bought a pony for 50 dollars of a man with the train
(25)

### September 10

About ten Oclock last night, a man on a mule came into camp with a note which said that the mail coach and a train was attacted by the indians. We saddled up and rode back on the road eight miles in short order. We found the train all right, and all the attact there had been was five indians came into camp, which scared them and they sent an express for us. We met a large number of the Appaches coming up today; they had one US horse which we took. We are camped just above a large boddy of Commanches

20 miles

### September 11

The indians in camp are as pleanty as graybacks on a gold miner, and they are all hungry as usual. A detale of twenty men left with five days rations to go and look for a camp of Texans which the indians say are on salt creek south of here. We are to remain here a few days. I made a trade for a horse with the Appaches today. He is a Texan horse. A great many of the Appaches are part Mexican and can speak the language, Los Comanchees tanbian.

I gave a pony that cost fifty dollars, and a rifle that cost fifteen for my horse

### September 12

The squaws are continualy begging for something to eat. This is not a very pleasant encampment for there is no wood and verry little watter

We have no tents, so we have to ly about in the hot sun all day, which is verry dissagreeable at the least. There are four tribes of indians or part of four tribes camped here on this river some above us and some below us

Arrappahoes, Comanchees, Appachees, and Kiawas

They are all friendly.

### September 13

The sun is as hot as ever, and the river as dry as a turnpike.

I paid vissit to the Comanche Camp today. I found noboddy at home but the squaws and old men. There are no warriers here, and I believe there are but few any way. I believe that this command composed of seventy mounted men and two pieces of cannon manned with twenty four men, is able to whip all the indians on this river were they disposed to fight us

There must be nearley three hundred lodges of them

### September 14

Alfred Ruyle[92] and I took a ride up the river today to the camp of Ten Bears a Commanchee Chief. He has been to Washington this summer and as a matter of course he had a great deel to tell about what he saw. He does not speak english but I managed to converse with him in Spanish

He says as they all do that he and his tribe are good men but the other indians are bad men

### September 15

There was considerable whiskey in camp this morning, which the boys got at a mexican train last night.

As soon as the squaws and indians, who came here to beg, discovered this, they made themselves verry scarce and have not been seene today since. I suppose they thought that the whiskey would make the boys quarrelsom and it would be better to keep away

Pritchard, Killmore and George Ayres[93] came in from below last night about midnight, and brought in a buffalo they had killed

### September 16

The boys who went below with Major Antony[94] and interpreter smith cam in to day. They have had a fuss with the Kiawas down below about a government mule, two of them drew their bows and fixed their arrows, but got knocked down as quick as a flash of lightning by Buccannon and Ferris,[95] and otherwise so roughly handled that they were glad to 'have some scence'. The matter was settled without any further difaculty

### September 17

Nothing to do but to lounge about camp in the hot sun. It is getting a little cooler nights now in fact it is uncomfortably cool some of these nights, especially toward morning. Killmore, (or Shyster), sat up till about twelve last night cooking some beans, and he made so much noise that noboddy could sleep in camp. When he got them cooked he went arround pulling the boys out of bed and inviting them to come and eat some of Shyster's beans. Last night was one of the many the boys will have to talk about.

*September 18*

Killmore, Jones, and myself went up the river about nine miles to an Appache camp

Poor Bear is the name of the Chief in command of it. He told us they had no ponies to spare that were good for any thing, so we went a mile farther up to the camp of Ten Bears a Comanche Chief we could not trade with him, but he liked to talk, and so we stayed till nearley night talking with him about his trip to Washington, by signs, a little spanish etc. He told me I would make a good Commanchee, and he would give me his daughter if I would join them

*September 19*

Have been lying about camp all day in the hot sun. some of us boys who never gamble have been trying to pass away the time by playing poker for gun caps, and we made it out verry well. The gambling in camp is not quite as brisk as it was, becaus a great many of the boys are broke: but there is considerable of it yet among the more fortunate

The Indians who were camped across the river from us have pulled up and moved farther down the river

*September 20*

There have been several indians of the Apache and Comanche tribes from the camps above here, in camp today

Ten Bears found my pipe which I lost in his camp the other day, and he brought it to me. As soon as he came in camp he enquired for me by the name of Comanchee

The pipe was broken and he has fixed it for me. He told the boys that I was a good Comanchee, and was going to marry his daughter. They of course made great sport of me on the head of it

*September 21*

I have been playing poker for Amuscitios again today, as the onley way to pass the time. Life is rather dull here as there is no game within reach, it being driven of by the indian camps. The onley recreation we have is games of cards and talking with the indians still this is a great deel better than like in quarters. I have been troubled with the rheumatism or something of the kind twice on this trip and I dont know what to do about it, I hope by all that is good I aint going to have that dissease the ballance of my life

*September 22*

Quite a large mule train passed here today on its way to mexico. Jones[96] and myself saddled up our horses and rode up to the crossing to pas away the time this afternoon. The indians were as thick as flies around the train, and as a matter of course, were verry hungry. The watter is beginning to come down the river now: there is running watter eight miles above here

*September 23*

Well we are still on the Arkansas river about a mile below the crossing of the Santa fee road[97] there is not much fun in lying in camp in such a place as this on the open planes by the side of a dry river and without wood, still ther is but little complaint. The buffalo chips are getting so scarce that we have to go two or three miles for them now. Our grub is getting scarce too. there is nothing but bread and and coffee.

It is rumored in camp that we are to leave here in the morning

*September 24*

We had revilee before day light this morning and breakfast soon after The pack up and saddle up were sounded and we got on the road again. I stopped at the Commanchee camp and bid good bye to my Indian Fatherinlaw we camped at noon for dinner and then travailed till near sundown

30 miles

*September 25*

Our grub is getting short but we met Hall[98] today with pleanty of provissions and forrage. We camped again for dinner and travailed again in the afternoon

25 miles

*September 26*

have been in the saddle all day on a light breakfast, We are consequently pretty hungry. We passed the Arrappaho camp about five miles below here. We are camped at the pleasant encampment again

40 miles

*September 27*

I was put on cook last night and consequently had to get up pretty early this morning. Revilee by moonlight, breakfast by moonlight, and a start by daylight this morning. Ely Msoure[99] brought an Antelope into camp this evening

There is the usual amount of cursing at the cooks, but I have got to be too old a soldier to get out of humor about it

30 miles

### September 28

Revilee, breakfast, and an hour on the road before daylight this morning. We travailed into Fort Lyon by twelve Oclock forty five miles. I went to find a place to board as soon as we got here, but did not succeed: for that reason I shall have to continue cooking as much as I dislike the business

45 miles

### September 29

We will have to come down to regular soldiering now, Lieut. Willson[100] is here and he has taken command of the company.

The orders are, rollcall three times a day and ever thing in style

The boys think it will play out in a few days however

We are now on the last year of our enlistment, and the boys are beginning to count the months and days from now till their time expires, and to look forward to the time of their discharge as the next thing to the millennial.

### September 30

The grub has pretty near played out

There has been nothing but coffee without suggar, and bread

We had some beans without bread, or coffee, or sugar for dinner

The boys have verry little grumbling to do on the account of the grub considering that they have good cause for complaint

The weather is fine through the day, but it is rather coole in the morning

### October 1

Oh! Who would'nt be a soldier? Who would'nt enlist to fight for his country? There is considerable pleasure in a soldiers life, as it is in this country at least. Our armey regulaitons or the way they are carried out or attempted to be carried out are a compleet sistem of despotism, by which a few small minded aspirants tyrannnise over the masses. If it were not for the fact that they are the only ones we have, and that the cause of liberty is worth more than all else, no true American could ever submit to the abuses and degredation of a private soldier

### October 2

I came off of cook today and as Jessie's resignation has been accepted he was put on in my place.

He has been winning considerable lately, and feeling pretty liberal he sent over to the store for a couple of bottles of champagne; this started the boys and they threw in around and sent for a box, and that giving out they sent for another, till a good many of the boys got pretty tight. It was amusing to see them staggering about feeling themselves the best men in the world, and in the best humor imaginable

They have spent between 300, and 400 dollars at the store today.

### October 3

The weather continues fine with cool nights and bright sunshiney days: but there is nothing to relieve the monotoney of camp life except such things as the *spree* of yesterday and there is no pleasure is *such* things for me and for that reason I never have anything to do with them.

Not that I am any too good or too morral to join in a drunken debauchee (if that is the word), oh no! I will not attempt to persuade myself to believe any thing of the kind: but as I said before there is no pleasure in such things for me, and therefore I do not join in them.

I am now on the last year of my enlistment and therefore I ought to begin to think of what I shall do when my time is out. I often ponder on this subject but can come to no conclusion. I have all along calculated to go home: but several times lately have I caught myself thinking of some other plan: for I like a great maney other youg men, do not like the idea, after leaving home to make a raise, seek my fortune, or whatever it may be called, of going back empty handed.

Yet on the other hand there is Mother, and Annie, and Albert and Ben whome I have not seene for over three years;-and it will be over four when my time expires; I *must* go home. I know that I can by industry and frugallity, as a farmer secure for myself an independance if not a competency: yet it seemes hard to leave to work hard for so many years in order to enjoy life when I get to old to appreciate or enjoy wealth

To enjoy life! What is it to enjoy life? Who knows? I certainly do not! I cannot remember a time when I was contented with my condition, since I was old enough to think about it at all: yet there are, or have been times upon which I look back with pleasure

Perhaps the verry life I am leading now: at which I am so impatient: when it becomes a part of the past, will be allso looked back to with pleasure. still I do not enjoy myself, nor have I since I was a soldier. I am not as discontented as I was the first six months, in fact I am not discontented at all scarcely. yet I am not contented; or rather I am contented with a kind of a forced contentment: resignation I suppose it is. There is one thing I have learned since I have been a soldier, and that is, not to be impatent of circumstances over which I have no controll

### October 8

I am on guard today There are four posts, and I am number four of the first relief. The numbers four do not walk post through the day, but guard the commissary during the night: consequently I have had nothing to do today, but will have to stand post at the commissary tonight

### October 9

I had to stand but two hours guard last night: therefore I consider I have had a very easy guard this time, for I only stood two hour for a whole twenty four hours guard, whereas generally I have to stand eight.

Some of the boys are getting ready to go to Fort union in escort of a train of eight hundred horses which came in from the states day before yesterday, If I had not been travailing so much this summer I should volunteere to go on this trip, for I would rather be on the road than in garrison any time

### October 10

was detailed on wood fatigue this morning and had to go and get a load of wood, or help get it.

Thirteen of the boys went with the train of horses this morning, and they turned us out of doors by taking our tent. My bunkey went, so I had to hunt another. I was luckey enough to find one in the person of Springer,[101] who had a bunk put up in the quarters. The quarters are in a better condition now than when we came in: there have been some doors and windows put in and the boys are putting up some bunks in them

### October 11

Sunday! A day only known to a soldier, as inspection day. Our weekly inspection used to be on foot: but lately it is on horseback; with all our arms and equpiments. And woe be it to him who is absent from it, without a good and sufficient excuse. I have passed the day in lounging about the quarters, and writing some letters to my friends, which I should have done long ago

### October 12

The weather is pleasant, and indeed warm in the middle of the day, but cold nights. The Arrappahoe Indians come about the post every day to beg and traffic: Their camp is a couple of miles below here. Our life here has settled down into its old monotony, as usual in posts. There is nothing to do but to stand an occasional guard, go on fatigue occasionally etc.

### October 13

Oh! Why did I not provide myself with usefull books when I first enlisted and put my spare time, which hangs so heavily on my hands: to some use.

Well I have asked myself the question and as nobody else will or can I will try an answer it. First I did not think of it, and if I had thought of it, I was not in a place where books were to be bought: novels I could have bought in denver: but they were of the wishey washey love and murder stamp mostly; but good books were scarce there at that time. And second if I had thought of it, or if they were to have been had, I did not at that time have any money, nor 'till twelve months after. So I could not have bought them either in denver or send for them by mail. But I shall never forgive myself for not sending for them this summer, though I have a slight excuse yet: I have been saveing my money to buy a horse and have but just mad out to do it, for what with the *little* I spent, and that that has been swindled out of me by loaning it out, I have had a hard time of it. I have thought of books several times this summer, but the hope of getting enough togather to buy a horse has kept me back.

Here has been two (and a little over) years of my life, and it is likley to be three, which has been wasted! Causes over which I had no controll (or but little) have combined to waste my time!

How many hours on hours have I thrown away in idle speculation, or fretfullness? Might I not have used in the storing my mind with usefull knowledge; Had I had the opertunity, or the inclination. Hours which can never be called back. I have often thought of these things, yet I have not used my *utmost* endeavers to make it otherwise.

Had I done so I might say that it is fate: and I am not to blame: but I have not: and consequently I am the one to blame fate has nothing to do with it. I have no doubt, but many, many, times, I have had opertunuties to get information, which I did not improve.

## October 17

I know that I have written a great many foolish—yes silly things in this book, and—well. what of it? What if I have? Who's business is it? Who's going read them? I am!

No! I don't know as I shall either! But if I dont, nobody shall! Tha'ts certain!

I aint going to have anybody criticising *my* writing!

Why! No good! As I know of, but that it has served as a pastime, and employment: and that is enough for a lot of trash like this to have done, or to do.

## October 18

This is the day which I could allways distinguish allways feel: as it were; at home: but here and in fact ever since I crossed the Missouri river, there has been no sunday: all are alike. I should not have known that today was sunday at all: only this evening when I took up my book to write a little in it, I saw the word sunday at the head of the page upon which I was just going to write.

We had our weekly inspection today: but that is all there is to remind one of the day of the week

## October 19

Monday! This was the day on which I used to commense my weeks work.

I used to think I ought to do a good days work, on monday any how. Those were the times when I worked hard and was contented. Yes, contented! I didn't know it then I thought I was'nt contented, but I was, perfectly contented: in comparrison to what I have been since, and much better contented than now: 'though I am better contented (resigned?) now, than I have been sometimes, a thousand times.

## October 21

I was too late for rollcall this morning, and had to go on fatigue in consequence

I was ordered to report to the Adgutents office at eight Oclock which I did. Four of us with a non-com were sent with two post teams down to the butcher shop to haul loggs for a corell. All we had to do in the world was to hitch a couple of loggs on to the hind axeltree of each waggon, and haul them about a quarter of a mile; and drink our regular fatigue whisky.[102] My share I gave to the other boys. And *this* is soldering: seven men and two six mule teams sent to do what one man and one team ought to do

### October 30

Last night I was sitting on my bunk sewing a pair of gloves, with a candle burning. There were some of the boys playing cards on the table, at the same time. About ten minits after tapps Searg't Jones[103] told the boys to put out their light and go to bed. They asked for the privailage of playing two more hands, but he told them to put it out: or go to the guard house; and ordered myself and Springer (my bunkey) to put on our arms, and take them there. I told him that I had a light also, and had as good a right to go, as they. Jones after several had refused to take us, found a couple of men to go with us and so put us in

I dont like this being in the guard house verry well though aside from the disgrace of the thing, we are as comfortable here as in the quarters

The old guard hous has been repaired, and we were moved there today. There are two rooms, one for the guard and one for the prisoners. Our room has no fire in it, so we have to stay in the guardroom through the day.

I was mustered in the guard house today as a prissoner, that is our regular muster day came today and I was mustered here. What would Mother say to that

I had hoped that as I had served over two years without being under an arrest, that I might serve my time out without it cant be helped now. Allthough there is something disgracefull in being a prissoner I feel that I have done nothing disgracefull or dishonorable: and I am confident I should not have been here, had I not had the misfortune to fall in the way of an idiot who happned to wear the shiveroones: which he uses as a means of careying out his own *idiotic* designs, of making as maney enemies as possible

### November 2

The snow has nearley all gone. there only remains a little in shadey places, but the ground is somewhat damp yet. Captain cook was Officer of the day, and he promiced to get us a stove for our room; but neglected to do so

### November 3

Four of us prisoners were sent to cut wood at the Adjutents office this morning. We hacked and hagled the wood up to the best of our abillity and then came away: leaving more chips than stove wood, and more notches than love behind us

### November 4

It has been rather cold and windy today. Seargent Jones has been in command of the guard, and has shown by being as accomodating as he could, a disposition to plaster over the fact that *he* is the caus of our confinement and disgrace.

He knows as well as I do, that we are here for nothing else, than becaus *he* wanted to show his authaurity. And *I* know as well as *he* does, that he is no *gentleman,* or he would not have taken *such* a mean low lived spite at us, without giving us an equal show

### November 5

The Office of the day released all of us, that is all of company F prissoners, at guard-mount this morning.

There seems to be pleanty of wine afloat among the boys today, if one is to judge by appearances

### November 6

I went to work and scoured up all my arms today, as the Captain has bought a fewe sheats of sandpaper, (at an expence of fifty or sixty dollars of the company fund, I presume) and as the ballance of the boys have cleaned theirs, It wont do for me to be behind in this respect, unless I wish to go to the guardhouse again

### November 7

There was a man from the states passed here a few days ago with two or three waggon loads of liquors. [*crossed out*] and by invitation of the officers, (it is said) he camped clost by, and was selling a tolerable article of native wine to the boys, at two dollars a gallon: to lighten his load he said. He was arrested last evening, and the officers are *confiscating* his load as fast as they can. It is said that two or three barrels of wine were confiscated unbeknown to the officers, before it was unloaded

*November 8*

We had a verry strict Company inspection this morning, and a dress parade this evening, at which there were several orders read: some from the head of the war department, some from the head of *this* department and some from the district head-quarters at denver. All of which were more tegeous [tedious] than interesting

*November 9*

We had company drill this morning, and battallion drill this afternoon: during which we made (our Co.) our usual awkward appearance in consequince of our officers being such egrigious blockheads, as to give the wrong commands, and throw us into confusion. I dont believe there is a private in the Co., but could learn either of the officers something about the drill. Lieutennant Akley[104] and the boys with him, came in from Fort Union while we were on drill

*November 10*

For some reason or other we had neither Co. nor battallion drill today. And although thirteen of the boys came in from a tripp last evening, I have not—as strange as it seemes, seene a drunken man, today or last night.

Blakey, All. Cockran, and myself took a ride about five mile up the river, this afternoon, for exercise

*November 11*

Today is my regular guard day. There was considerable wine found its way into our quarters, and down the throats of the boys, by some unaccountable means or other today: the most of whom were in a decidedly mellow state about the middle of the afternoon. It has a verry different effect however, from the rott that the boys generally get hold of: for instead of their all wanting to fight and bruise each other, as usual, they are in the best humor immigginable

Where the wine comes from, is more than I know: *perhaps* it is some of that the officers *confiscated*, and the boys *controbanded*.

*November 12*

The Paymaster arrived here last evening, and he has paid off the troops in this post today.

Gambling has commenced again, with all its usual vigor.

It is courious that men *will*, as soon as they get a little money, always go to work with such feverish hast to get rid of it as fast as possible and never rest easy untill the last "scad" has disappeared.

But such is the case, and allways will be the case I suppose. Some are 'broke' allready, and others will be in a day or two, while a *few* will win the other's money, and then spend it with the greatest profusion

### November 13

Friday is mail day and I have forggotten to write letters, untill it is to late, for another week to send them

This spirit of procrastination is a verry common thing with me, and for some reason or other the less I have to do, the more I put it off for the morrow

### November 18

[*Entry is indecipherable*]

### November 21

I am on guard again today. The guard will be heavier on us now that our garrison is diminished. The weather has been fine for some time, but there are heavy clouds lowring up in the east this evening, which look verry much like a storm of some kind before morning.

It looks exactly as it did the evening before the last snowstorm when I was on guard as I am now and on post at the hay stack the same as now

### November 22

Mike Hollenbeck[105] went to work yesterday and put up a small wall tent to live in because the quarters are so cold damp and unhealthy: and he sais I may come and live with him.

It comencid snowing about two Oclock last night and has continued all the forenoon. We were relieved from guard at 9 this morning, by the new guard reporting at the guardhouse, instead of mounting guard in the regular way. Two of the Co's. of Missouri Vol'ts which passed here a few weeks ago, came in from Union in the storm today. they look about as Co. F usually do about these stormey times

### November 23

I bought a bunk of John Ferris, and moved into the tent with Mike today. We have a small sheat iron stove but it smokes like damnation

It has been a blustering disagreeable day

*November 24*

We did not sleep the warmest last night, but we have put our bedding togather and will try if it is not more comfortable sleeping togather. We have made a bargain to take turns building a fire mornings

The weather has turned off clear as a whistle but cold

*November 25*

These Missouri boys are some of them pretty sociable they have some pretty hard stories to tell about the guerilla warfare in Missouri.

All of which are no doubt true. One of them fell behind the day they came in, and it was feared he was frozen; as his horse was found, and he was not, until today. He had lain out one night in the snow without blankets, and had frozen his feet. He has been stopping at the camp of a train since the first night

*November 26*

Mike and I bought a half bushel of frozen apples, which go verry well baked in our stove

*November 27*

It was Mikes turn to build a fire this morning, and he did not get up early enough to get the tent warm before stable call, and I did not wake up till the bugle sounded.

I jumped out of bed and comenced dressing: the tent was full of smoke, I coul'dnt find my clothes, my boots wire [were] frozen, I couldn't see or breathe, and withall I had an agreeable time of it: at last I got half dressed, and rushed out onley to find myself too late for rollcall: for which I was ordered into the guardhouse

The only way I had of getting out of it was to go on sick report. Which as I have such a cold as to be hardly able to speak was not hard to do

*November 28*

As I have got on the sick report, I shall remain on it a few days: 'though I should not have went on had it not been for the guardhouse. There is nothing the matter with me, but a pretty severe cold, for which I should not consider it worth while to [go] on the sick report, as a general rule

*November 29*

We got an old castiron cookstove today which does not smoke: so that we are more comfortable

*November 30*

Several of the boys have been busy all day, getting off for Pueblo: where they are to remain during the cession of the court. The weather is a little more moderate today. The wood gave out at the quarters, and the boys have been standing about in their overcoats uttering all sorts of curses and imprecations, while Mike and I are as comfortable in our little tent, with our little stove filled with wood of our own getting, (over the river) as two bugs in a rug

*December 1*

The weather still grows more mild: in fact it has thawed a little today, enough to soften the snow so it does not squeak

*December 2*

I did not go to the hospital at the sick-lame-and-lazzy call this morning, so I suppose I am reported for duty. Its all right if I am for I am able to do duty, if I have got a little cold, which by the way is better than it was: and that is the reason I di'dnt go to sick call

*December 3*

Have done nothing but ly in the tent and read novells all day. Which is if any thing, is a little worse than doing nothing

*December 4*

This is my birthday and my guardday: consequently I may be said, to be supposed to fill this page with some nonsense or other, whether there has been anything transpired worth being cronicled er not.

I suppose,—if I hai'nt—lost a few years in my 'log', I and [am] twenty six today! Yes, twenty six! Though a mere boy yet! Yes, I feel that I am a mere boy yet! In mind, in experience, in everything but years and hard work!

Yet, shall I live to be a man? And if so, how many years longer shall I be a boy? Ah! Tha'ts it! At what age do we pass from boyhood to manhood? Twenty six years old! It dont seeme possible I can be that old!

*December 5*

I came off guard at 8° Oclock this morning.

Have been doing nothing with all my might ever since. Doing nothing is about the hardest work I ever did; and although I have had a considerable practice at it, I have not learned to do it with a good grace yet: and I don't know as I ever shall: though I can do it better than a couple of years ago. For if I dont do it with more patience than then, I am sure I do it with greater resignation at least.

The weather is getting warmer, and although the ground is still covered with snow, it is a good deel softer.

### December 6

The thaw has progressed to such an extent, that there are quite large patches of bare ground and considerable puddles of water: making it rather sloppy being out.

I cant say exactly that I have been doing nothing all day, for this is my fatigue day.

I had to go to the bakery and get a card of bread[106]

### December 7

We had inspection on foot this morning under full arms, by Maj' Dourning[107] the inspector Gen'l of this district. And *inspection* this afternoon mounted: under full arms and equipments.

So that what with the numerous roll calls, and *inspections*, I can not complain of anui today

### December 8

Notwithstanding the inspector General is still here, we have had no inspections today! Neither have we had drills

The boys over at the quarters still keep up their gambling, allthough it is not carried on with the viggor with which it was five days after payday, from the fact that a great many of the small fry are broke: but the more fortunate are now gambling with those of the same class in K Company. Poker is the principal game played now

### December 9

I have eat my usual meals, taken care of my horse, passed as much time as possable in pleasant conversations, and as much as I could not dispose of otherwise in my tent: and so worried out another day. I have wished a thousand times that I was, or had the faculty to be a musetion: so that I might while away some of my *waste* time with some instrument, as my nest door neighbor Whitiker does. *He* is a fiddler: and he will set an fiddle from morning till night, the verry personification of contentiment

While I have nothing to do but think! *Think! Think! Think!*

### December 10

If I had the power of language to express one half of what courses through my brane, I would write such a book about the life of a soldier, as should change the armey regulations, and the whole sistem of armey dicipline, and government, so that a Soldier would no longer be as he is, but a *man*: in the full scence of the term and an Officer would have to be a man, or else no Officer. If I could do that, I would consider that I had done more for humanity, than any other man who had lived on the earth, and I should die perfectly contented with myself, and believing that I was not borne for naught.

### December 11

And once again am I on guard! Though I cant say as it is verry hard, to go on duty once in a while; but I must say, it does rile a feller *some*what to be on post without a gun with orders to halt all persons comeing near, and demand the cuntersign for fear that it might be the Officer of the day slipping up to catch you napping

Which if he ever does, ther'is no doubt of his slapping you into the guard house, in less than notime at all hardley

### December 12

If a fellow is obliged to write something every day, and each day is so much like the others, that he cannot write the incidents of the day, without repeeting every day what he has written the day before, what in the name of common (scence?) will he work out of his brain to write? Today has been just like all the other saturdays when I am in a post, am not on guard, or have no other duty to do.

### December 13

The weather continues about the same: freezing nights about as much as it thaws days, and perhaps a little more.

Of all the self imposed jobs, I ever had to do, this every day writing is the hardest. But! I have managed the thing along so far, and I guess I can contrive the ballance some how.

*December 14*

The boys over in the correlle, (quarters) are standing about one fire with their overcoats, on most of the time. The weather is not so verry cold, but it seems colder inside of those stone walls, than out doors: and the boys wont keep up a good fire. Mike and I are as comfortable as we can wish, and we would be contented if we had some means of passing away the time.

*December 15*

The wind blew up a small flurrie of snow from the east today

*December 16*

The weather turned around a little colder last night. A cold cutting north wind all day. It did'nt have much effect on us though, for we hav'nt to go out much unles we chose to; there being no drills, or inspections comeing off nowadays.

*December 18*

I have nothing to write today except that I am on guard and number four of the second relief.

I have to wait on the prissoners through the day, and go to the commissary at night.

*December 19*

We came down from the commissary at day light this morning

This has been the easiest guard I ever stood in this post; We only slept at the commissary but stood no post

*December 20*

I went on cook this morning again. I find that the cooking is much easier now than when I was on before, as in addition to the fireplace in the cookroom, there is a large cookstove now, and besides there are not as many to cook for

*December 21*

Tomey[108] and I got the regular meals for the boys which they demolished in their usual vigorous style making their usual number of (witty?) remarks about "The old farmer", "Peter Hurdle", and so forth being 'cook', 'slush', 'pot walloper', and the like.

I made a bargain with Frazier[109] to go on wood fatigue in his place, and he is to cook in mine after today.

*December 22*

Frazier went into the cookhouse in my place this morning, but I have not had to go after any wood yet; owing to the boys, having let their team run away and smash their waggon. They have turned it in and got another however, and will go after wood tomorrow

*December 23*

Harper[110] and I have been cutting wood this forenoon: but I have done nothing this afternoon, except that I played a game of freezeout, with George Pierce,[111] for a couple of cans of oysters on christmas, and another for a pound of crackers. He is to get the oysters, and I the crackers.

*December 24*

We went out and cut a couple of loads of wood again this forenoon. There was a heavy icey mist filled the air this morning and all the forenoon.

Lieutenant Wilson, and the boys got back from Pueblo this evening

The boys seem to be in fine spirits, and to have enjoyed their trip verry well. There are three or four of the boys at Pueblo, retained as witnessis in George Cook's case

*December 25*

Christmas today, is every where cellebrated but here. Some of the boys are cellebrating the day by getting 'tight', but as a general thing there is no notice taken of it.

George Pierce and I have concluded to have our oysters on New years day. Last night some of our Officers (Those moddles of propriety) were arround to the quarters, waking every boddy up to 'take a drink'.

Jim Boies[112] moved his bedding into our tent today so there are three of us now.

*December 26*

Last night, Jim Boies, All. Cochran, Bill Kaillinore, and some of the other boys got it into their heads that they must have some thing to eat. So they went over to the Sutller's and got six cans of oysters and a bottle of schnapps. They brought them to our tent, sending me after some milk, they got up a splendid oyster soupe: and there was eating and drinking in our tent, 'till a late hour in the night. And then to cap all, Jim "wanted some-thing to eat"! so he went to the store, roused them up and got another can of oysters. These he eat and went to bed. A good many still keep drunk, and more keep tight.

### December 27

The boys, Jim in particular, couldn't get along, without another oyster soupe again last night, but we got to bed at a more reasonable season, than the night before. The boys are begining to sober up today.

In fact, I havent seene either a drunken man, or a tight one all day.

I guess Christmas is over for this time, though it has been rather a meagre one here, and dry too: judging from the quantity of water demanded to quench thirst:

### December 28

The wood waggon crossed the river, and hauled over some wood we cut there on saturday, but by some reason, the boys went off without me: so I have had nothing to do all day.

Every thing has quieted down into the old course of things. There is no whiskey afloat, and gambling has nearley "dried up". Only to comence again next pay day, however!

### December 29

Harper, Winches, and myself went about a mile above here and cut a green cottonwood this morning. It is six foot through at the but and the top of it will make four loads of wood: two of which the boys hauled this forenoon. About four inches of snow fell last night, and the weather is quite cold today.

We had a kind of a dress par'ade in our quarters this afternoon, at which there were some orders read about the bounty offered by government for those who enlist in the veteran corps

### December 30

The weather is quite cold. So much so as to caus large iciales to freize upon the whiskers and mustaches in half an hour.

We cut and hauled the remaining two loads of wood upon that treetop. There is considerable excitiment in camp, about reenlisting in the veteren corps. I guess there will but few reenlist however I dont know what I shall do about it myself yet. We have untill the fifth of Jan. to make up our minds about it. I hope to get a letter or two friday. If I do, I shall know what to do.

*December 31*

The weather continues to be stinging cold. but clear

Well! Now my little book you have followed me through all the vicicitudes of ten months and two days of a soldiers life, and I must bid you, good bye! I know I have not done you that justice which your—before unspotted—pages demanded. I am concious that I have confided to you many foolish, silley things; for which I beg your pardon: and hoping I may do better by your successer, than I have by yourself, I now bid you a long farewell

Romine H. Ostrander
Co. F 1st Cav. of Colorado

*Fort Lyon, Feb 16th '64*[113]

Dear Mother!

Not knowing what better to do with this book, I have concluded to sent it to you, knowing that you can excuse my little discrepencies better than any boddy else. I will not attempt to excuse any of my acts as herein confessed, nor my maner of writing them down. I leave it all to you just as it is, and trust to a mother's affection for my excuse.

Acquainted as you are with my maner of writing, as well as my disposition and temperament, you can easily see my whole life as it passed before me in the year eighteen hundred and sixty three.

I received a letter from you last friday, dated Jan 24th. It is the first letter I have rec'd from home since Jan 16th, when I rec'd one from Albert. I rec'd one from Ben the same day I got yours. You want me to give you a discription of Fort Lyon. Perhaps you will find an attempt at one in this book elsewhere but no matter! I will try it any how.

Fort Lyon was built in July 1860 by Cos. F, G, H, and K, First U.S. Cavalry, under the command of Capt. Chadwick[114] (now a General of some kind I believe). It is situated on the left bank of the Arkansas river,[115] about one hundred and ten miles below Pueblo,—an old Mexican settlement at the mouth of the Fountainquiboul,—and which is mentioned in Fremont's reports,[116] and about thirty-eight or nine below Bent's old Fort. It is just above Bent's new fort, which the government has leased for a commissary for the post. It is built on a low flat bottom close to the river. It is merely a parade ground surrounded by the buildings. There is a row of four square correlles on the south sid of the parade ground which axis towards the river, each capable of containing an hundred horses, which are ranged arround the inside of the correlles in dirt-roofed stalls. Those correlles are built of stone and mud. The walls are about two and a half feet thick and ten feet high. It looks like one correll on the outside but is partitioned off into four by stone walls. Down the river east from these correlles is and about 100 feet from them another similer one built for a quartermaster's correlle. On the east side of the parade ground, and on a line with the east end of the four Company corrells, is a row of three quarters built of stone and mud, each about 150 feet long 30 wide and ten high, with a dirt roof and ground floor. The north end of each of these buildings is partitioned off with a stone wall for an orderly seargents room. The ballance of each building is one huge room, or "correlle," as we call it, and is calculated to hold a Company of soldiers. The south end of each being the kitchen. Each one of the quarters contains three fireplaces besides the kitchen fireplaces, which is a little larger than the others. Most of the Cos. here have their quarters partitioned off into smaller rooms with canvas gunnysacks and so forth. Our Co. have in this way four rooms besides the Orderlie's room. On the north side of the parade ground is a row of eight buildings of the same material as the others. They are about forty feet square are divided into two compartments, and each compartment into two rooms. These are the officers quarters. The west side is just like the east. On a line with the south end of the quarters on the east side is a row of stone buildindings five or six in number containing two rooms each. These are laundress quarters. This row runs east and west and is opposite to the quartermasters correlle. Just back of these is the post office and farther back (north) is the suttler's store, which is built of posts set in the ground chinked and mudded. It is dirt roofed. On the west side of the post on a line with the north side of the correlles is another row of landress' quarters running west.

Co. F ocupies the first one of the Co. quarters from the river on the west side, and their horses ocupy the second correlle from the west end of the corrells. The stage station is east of the suttlers store.

This post was formerly called Fort Wise[117] after some officer in the regular army. This Wise turned traitor and the name of the post was changed to Lyon as a tribute to the gallant General Lyon who was killed in Missouri at the head of his men.

The commissary, or Bents new Fort, is just below here on a hill that is a part of the bluff which comes down to the river. It is built of flat stones and mud the same as this post. It is built after the style of most houses in New Mexico, being a solled wall of rooms arround a plasa or square. There are two entrances: one on the east for teams, and one on the north for people.

The nearest farm or ranche is Bent's, at the mouth of the Purgatory[118] (which is pronounced Picket wire) or Las Animas (those demons) river. It is about twenty-three miles above here. There is quite a settlement on the Purgatory at the base of the Ratton Mountains about 130 miles south west from here, which is called Trinidad. There are other ranches on the stream scattered along at intervals. The nearest settlement on this river above Bent's old fort excep the stage station, which is on spring bottom, is Mr. Hanee's ranch, which is about seventy-five miles above here. The general face of the country above here is one continuous dry rolling prairie covered with grama grass. There is no timber in sight except the cottonwood on the river bottom. Pikes Peak and the Spanish Peaks are visable from a short distance from here on the high prairies.

April first 1864. I had written this far with the intention of sending it off by the next mail, but neglected to do so then, so will send it now. Your son,

Romine H. Ostrander

*This book
is the propety of
ROMINE H. OSTRANDER
of
Co F, Vet. Batt. 1st Col. Cav.*

*You will
confer a favor, by
returning it
to
him.*

### January 1, 1865

A sunshiney pleasant day! Snow rapidly disappearing! I am still in the Hospital as an Attendant! Have charge of the Convelescents room! There are seventeane patients in this room, but none of them are verry bad. Saunders who has the rheumatism is the worst case. He has to be lifted about. Mr. Vereling is an old man. He has some fever, appears to be slowly declining but may possibly never recover. Mr. Elder is blind, has a film over his eyes, may possibly regain his eye sight: blindness caused by the Gonorea settling in his eyes. Have two assistants to help me!

Hav'nt seene or heard anything of Santaclaus! Went to church this evening. The exercise turned out to be a sunday school concert. Nauggins[119] went with me.

### January 2

Another warm day! Rather sloppy under foot! Didn't sleep much last night! Too much noise! Couldn't! Sleep close to a window which opens uppon the street! Drunken fellows kept coming along, hallooing and fireing off pistols! Am going to load my pistol, and keep it under my head, and let some of them have its contents, if they don't quit it! Soldiers ought to know enought to respect a hospital if they *are* drunk: but if they don't they ought to be learned! 5 Oclock! Weather getting cooler!, guess t'will freeze tonight. Well! I have contrived to fill up two pages of this diary tolerably well. Wonder if I can manage to fill the other 363 pages!

### January 3

Ground froze this morning, and allthough the sun is out as bright as ever it has scarcely got the top of it slipery yet at eleven. People are moving about the streets as if they had busines on their minds. Loads of wood coming in, Gents riding on horse back and in buggies, men on foot, teamsters cracking their whipps, wagons rattling etc etc.

Went up town to the Ag't's office and to the P.O. Got a letter from Albert.

Tom. Young left today and he has not brought back Bonsers gloves,[120] which I loaned him. Wonder if he means to 'play me out' of them! The news is that Col' Moonlight, or Moonshine or Something, will be here in a day or two, to take comand of this district

### January 4

It is just one year since I signed my name to my Vet. Enlistment papers

They were made out, for the first of this month but were not signed until the fourth. I wonder if I shall have to serve the other two years! Or will the War close sooner! If they passe off as pleasantly as the last year has, I shall have no objections to serving my time out. I would rather the war would sooner however

A couple of howitzers were got out and tried in front of the hospital this morning. Col'l Moonlight has ariv', and Col'l Chivington has been mustered out. So sae's the Evening paper.

Believe I feele a little kind of sort of homesick but don't know!

### January 5

Could'nt sleep good! Those Baccallian soons [sons] of B— Sea Cooks, kept up their usual seranade, varied with an accasional bonebardment of firecrackers untill about one oclock this morning. A light snow fell to the depth of about two inches during the night. Have been reading a coppy of the Atlantic monthly all day whenever I could get a few minits time

Weather rather cold but clear and bright. Have loaded my revolver with powder and paper wadds, and intend to try and see "what virtue there is in grass", to disperse those streets mobbs which congregrate here and keep us awake nights

### January 6

Weather rather cold! I got a letter from Charlie

He writes a good letter: much better than I had expected

I got up about seven, had breakfast at eight, took a smoke, dressed the wounds, took my list into the dispensary and got the powders and medicins ordered, gave the doses, read about half an hour, then redd Charlies letter, took my dinner, sat down and answered it, gave the doses, read a little, went to supper, took a smoke went into the dispensary and had a game of cribbage[121] with the stewards, gave the doses, dressed the wounds, took a smoke, and went to bed.

This is about a sinopsis of every day and hour, varied by getting drinks of watter etc etc etc.

### January 7

Those baccalian sons of King Adherball[122] saw fit to congregate at the saloon opposite list [last] night about half past twelve, and make nois enough to wake the seven sleepers: or if not them, the sick sleepers of the hospital at any rate. I raised the window and opened a brisk fire upon them of paper wadds masked battery.[123] This caused a panic in their ranks and they re-treated precipotatly in all directions. Some towards camp weld and some toward town, where I presume they have taken up new positions: but as I didn't follow them I positively can't say but some of them are running yet.

### January 8

The weather continues quite cold, and there is a light sheet of snow on the ground the most of which fell last night. Another man—one of the bloody third,[124] who belongs to the hospital, was arrested this morning on the charge of stealing a trunk full of clothing. I have not been out of the house but once today and then only to go onto the next street after my jacket, and right back. Col'l Moonlight has begun to show his disc [discipline] by releasing the greater share of the provost guard, and by prohibiting soldiers coming into town without a pass.

They say "the Indians have murdered a dozzen men down below, and that The coach containing a paymaster with heavy funds, was robbed.

### January 9

Terry was released this morning being innocent. He said they took him out last night and threatened to shoot him, at the same time placing a cocked revolver to his head, if he didn't tell where the stolen clothing was. As he didnt know, of course he couldn't tell.

They then put a rope around his neck and over a limb and choked him a little. He couldnt tell and so they released him. If innocent men are to be served in this manner, I dont know how soon *I* shall look over a limb myself.

The only shaddow of suspicion that there was against Terry was that he went after his washing to a house near the place from which the trunk was stolen

Any of us are liable to in the neighborhood of a theft at any time in this country

### January 10

The weather has somewhat moderated: so that it is somewhat sloppy in the middle of the road. Captain, or rather Major Logan[125] is getting up a co. of independent citizens to go after the Indians.

I signed my name to a petition to Col'l Moonlight, asking him to send a squad of us Vets, under the command of Seargent Fribley, along with Logans Co. There is considerable excitement here about the Indians again. They have been committing more depridations on the platt. Julesburgh[126] is evacuated, and the stage line stock taken somewhere else. A train has been robbed, also a coach. Some soldiers and cittizins had a fight with Indians and killed over fifty. Provisions are going up.

### January 11

Patients are increasing on our hands lately pretty fast. Measles seems to be the complaint of the most of our new ones

This room is now filled up with the exception of one bed.

Wrote a letter and sent to Albert fifty dollars. Logans Co. are some of them backing out. Hain't heard anything of our petition. Guess Moonshine does not intend to take any notice of us poor satelites.

No dinner! Chief cook is up town on a bender, and under cooks don't know what to cook. Vereling is getting better: he went down to the dining room for his supper.

Wish I was with Co. F, and out after Indians or somebody else! Getting tired of one thing all the time. Better than doing nothing though!

### January 12

Mobbs in the street again last night who made night hideous with their yells.

Don't like it! Wish these brothell houses of h–l were burned down! Either the hospital ought to be moved, or these nests of polution rased to the ground. There are a couple of howitzers close by, standing outside at the ordinance warehouse, and were it not for the danger to human life, I would steal them some of these nights, and send a couple of loads of through and through this nest of polution. Ain't quite sure but I shall be tempted to do it anyhow!

No news from the states now. The tellegraph operator at Julisburg has left and consequently there is noboddy to switch off the news for us.

*January 13*

Some of our old patients have been sent away, and new ones have taken their places. Evry bed in my room is now full. Some more of the Sand creek wounded have come in.

The weather is rather cold, but not extreemely so. Dont hear any more about Logans Indian expidition. I guess it's "played out"! The tellegraph is all right again, for some reason or other. Guess the Julesburg operator has got to his post again. Strange the Indians dont destroy it! Been looking at my algebra a little today. Can't see in to the pesky thing! Simple divission bothers me! Guess Iv'e forgotten the most I ever knew about it! Don't know what else can be the matter.

*January 14*

Two weeks of the new year have nearly gone by and it is getting quite natural for me to think of 1865 as the present year

A part of a large train which has been making up for the states, rolled out today. There will be over a hundred waggons in it when it is all made up. They have the same old cast iron six pounder, which our Co brought up from the Arkansas river, the fall of 1860.

The one we found hidden is a cornshock, and which we loaded with ounce balls for the benefit of an immaginary foe who were to attack us and rescue the forty one prisoners, we were bringing from Ft Wise to Denver

*January 15*

I remained in the house all day, but went to church at seven oclock this evening.

Father Keeler visited us this afternoon, and read one of his long prayers: or rather long string of prayers. The weather is stinging cold this evening

What is the power of expressing thought? Is it a natural quallification? Or, is it an aquired power, the result of propper education! If the former, why am I not endowed with it? And if the latter, Why may not I acquire it? I sometimes have Ideas in my head which I cannot express. I wonder if all men have not such ideas? Or are my Ideas in such an imperfect state, as to be inexpressable

*Is* my brane so muddy as to be incapable of one clearly defined original idea? I should'n't wonder! All of us can't be geneouses!

### *January 16*

The day has been usualy quiet with us, but there is some excitement on the streetes, caused by various flying rumors about the Indians down the platt.

A great many of them are no doubt true, and probably as many are false or colored.

All are lisened to with a somewhat incredulous care, instead of being eagerly swallowed as was the case last fall: and few are believed, unless substanciated by good authority. I think that nothing less than an attact on the place would caus such a consternation as existed here in aug'

A false allarm, followed by undue excitement, is unquestionably a bad thing! But incredulity acompanied by appathy, is decidedly worst in a time of danger! Dont know whether there are being any stringent measures taken to "go for 'em" or not!

### *January 17*

Streetes a little sloppy, but not to be compared in that respect to Illinois, and scarcly to be mentioned on the same day. I was sumonsed as a witness before Esquire Hall, to testify what I knew about the dance house across the street from here. I believe the proprietor was fined ten dollars and costs. If there is any *justice* in such a sentance, I "can't see it"

Bed time! Have just been reading the evening news! Tellegraph is all right; More Indian fighting down below the Junction.[127]

I wish our reg't was as full as they were once, and all here in denver. Oh! Wouldn't we go for 'em with a vegence!

I dont know as I am a verry brave man; but I should like to go on such an expidition, withe the first of three years ago

### *January 18*

A splendid sheat of snow fell last night to the depth of about four inches.

Patients all doing well, and every thing goes on fineally

Last winter at this time I was on wood fatigue every day, and the pages of my diary cronicled incidents which each day chipped out of the greene cottonwoods around fort Lyon. Now, it is different!

Each page is dressed with the bandiges taken from the wounded limbs of a life in a hospital, and dosed with the powders and extracts, put up and sent in, from the surgery of-living-in-a-house-and-never moving-out-of-it, which are ordered by the assistant Surgeon

Fill-a-page-if-it-takes-a leg-off, or, Nonscence-is-better than-no-scence.

### January 19

Col' Moonlight is said to be doing a good service, in ferriting out those parties who have had "a good thing" for the past two or three years here, in the way of perquisites; or on other words, who have been in the habbit of making money out of our dear old Uncle,[128] when his back was turned, by selling forage, rations, clothing, Indian horses, and every thing in fact, they could get their hands on.

He has found out more of these "good things", since he has been here, than Chivington would have done for a year to come. "A new broom sweeps cleane", and I hope this ray of moonshine will continue to illuminate the dark corners 'till there is not a nest of these Vamphires left unexposed.

"Go in Moonlight!!"

### January 20

A light downey snow has been falling all day; quietly, gracefully, noislessly, gloriausly!!

Just such a snow storm as one delights in! One that brings up dellightfull memories of the past, with all their trooping scenes of merriment and happiness. Days that alass, are past and gone, and can never be lived over again, except through the medium of that blessed ever present companion, and mentor, the *memory*.

And is this not one of our greatest sourses of happiness that we can look back on scenes, in which we did not realise our enjoyment freely at the time, with delight!

I think it is! At least I would'nt loose mine for worlds! For I am of such a nature, that I never enjoy the present properly.

### January 21

Still snowing! Verry lightly, meagerly! With a harder, rounder, colder prisistance. As if 'twere half a mind to quit, but still filt bound to keep on till it's power wore out and the relief came around.

How can a fellow help thinking of his first pair of scates, his many expiriences on the hillside with the sled. or the many times he went through the old swamp or across mister Sawtells pasture to school; such weather as this I should like to know? And if he should be reminded of the winter in the mountains, with Fred. and Henry, 'twouldnt be at all surprising.

Hard cider, luscious apples, walnutts, chestnutts, and hickorinutts, all claim their memory.

George! I wish I had some this evening!

### *January 22*

A verry cold day! Snow about eight inches deep and we have verry little woods! What there is is green cottonwood, and it makes a verry cold fire. Boys stand around the stoves in a fruitless attempt to keep them warm.

We managed to borrow a little wood this evening, but not half enough to keep us warm. Father keeles visited us again this afternoon. I havn't been out of the house during the past week, except once, when a provost came after me as a witness. Rather hard business finding matter to fill a page when one does not move out of one room from one day's end to another and when ones duties of a day are stereotyped to be used on each sucseeding day, ad infinitum.

### *January 23*

Gallaher and Cassidy[129] called on us this morning and stayed 'till in the afternoon; and Mr. Metzler[130] dropped in a little while also. Still cold! Twenty degrees below zero, or fifty two below freezing at daylight. The boys managed to get a little wood today, so that we have been comfortable. The soldiers (recruits and straglers) at camp, have no wood this cold weather, and they are in rather a bad condittion in those old dilapidated quarters

Oh! The poor private soldiers. How he is fostered and cared for! Furnished with every thing the heart could wish, clothing, rations, quarters, and pleanty of money, What has he to complain of! "Who would'nt be a soldier??" "Who would'nt fight for his country??"

### *January 24*

A nice cold, frosty, bright, pleasant day! I took a walk up town this afternoon. People were sterring about briskly, the snow squeaking under their feet merrily; making a scene lively, and exilirating.

No mail! Verry little news by tellegraph! Two new patients.

Alb is staying here with us for a few days. I have pretty spirited arguments with these third reg't ducks sometimes about the barbarity of indiscriminantly murdering defenseless women and children of the Indians at sand creek. Some of them deny that any thing of the kind was done except in the general action when there was no telling the difference; and some acknowledge that there were women and children killed after the general action was over; but argue that it was right because Indians have done the same

### January 25

Still cold! No mails, no news no nothing of the outside world except our regular evening tellegrams which we read with all the more eagerness, not knowing but each will be the last. I slipped down into the court room close by, to see what the cittizens were going to do about organising into malitia Cos. There were only about twenty or thirty present: one of them was holding forth about the fright and inconsintancy of any body but himself at the time of the other scare.

Among other things he spoke of a man who he said came into his house and reported 800 indians on the cut off and said he kicked him out of the house. You lie! Came from the crowd. No sir! That's the truth! And I want you to take that back! walking briskly across the room. I dont lie! You did *not* kick me out of the house, Said one as he reached him a mark on the chick

### January 26

Still cold but a little more moderately so this afternoon.

When a fellow has things crawling through his head, which allthough they may be of verry little consquence, he is to lazy to comb out, and spread before the eyes of his egotism, upon the pages of a diary, or too thick brained and languageless, to be able to put them in a propper form to suit his ambitions fancy, What buiness has he to pay out two and a half for so foolish a thing as a book like this, I'd like to know! None Whatever! Had better save his money for the christianization of scescescionestes or the relief of coloradothirdoters!

### January 27

The principal topic of conversation with us today is that Dr. Smith has been ordered to Ft Lyon. Which fact has been discussed in all it's bearings possable or impossable by all hands all day. It is said the reg't has been consolidated and that six of co F were attached to some other co than the one the main part of the co. was attached to. Hope I aint one of the six, for I shouldn't feele at home in any other co.

Doctor Hamilton is to be in charge here, and Beatty[131] is to be steward, or Robinson is going to Fort Lyon that being the H'd Dr's of the first Vet'. Cav of Colorado for the present. We have ceased to be a reg't and are only a battallion now.

### January 28

More moderate! In fact, a little thawish. Business is business, and things is workin got a letter from Henry and answered it.

He has some idea of farming next summer and some idea of enlisting shouldn't be at all surprised if he does neither

Some of those sons of Bachus got to hollerin again last night and I gave them the last wad in my Ravol-batery[132] which broke a window out of the saloon opisite. The saloon keeper came over this morning and wanted to know who did it: but no one could tell but me, and I wouldn't, he did'n't find out

### January 29

Did'n't go to Church or any where else. Father Keeler made his usual call this afternoon, and favored us with his usual prays. I am allways glad to see the old gentleman, and would have no objection to his calling on us a little oftener, for he is allways agreeable, and probably sincere in his religious belief, allthough he has a quere way of showing it. Dr. Hamilton took charge of the sick and wounded today, the latter of whom he give a general probing all around, with not a verry gental hand. I felt allmost like hitting him myself when he probed Frank Parks' leg, he was so rough about it.

### January 30

The people are enrolling all the able boddied men in town and organising them for the defence of the place. "Sand creek on the brain", "Indians on the brane", and "High officials", on the brane, are getting to be fearfully prevelent diseases in these parts about these times. The wire is out of fix somewhere below the Junction, so we can get no tellegrams from the states: there is verry little or no mail, and consequently, us poor bedenvered mortals are driven uppon our own entrench resources for topics of conversation, and there is no wonder that every partical of new especially Indian news is eagerly gobbled up and made the most of

### January 31

A mild but not verry pleasant day, in consequence of the fact that it has been rather sloppy under foot.

The softness of the walking has'n't hindered the news maker in bis. much I guess: for there are all kinds of rumors of Indian fighting. down the platt, Here is a specimen or two. Lieu't Kennedy is surounded by Indians on all sides and has a fight every day! His amunition is out and he has tellegraphed for more. Lieut' Walters is in the same fix and the train he is in escort of have lost 500 head of cattle. There are three thousand Indians on the other side of the river below the Junction.

### February 1

All quiet on the streets: Two coaches came in from the states but brought no mail. There is no news except Indian news, and that is getting to be about as believable as the story of the mountain of gold, or the arabian knights tale

There were three or four pistol shots heard in the neighborhood about dark, and about fifteen minits after, a man was brought in here with a ball hole through his thigh.

He was a little tight', and didn't appear to mind it much, walking about and talking more than I should think a man with a hole through his leg could. Twas some kind of a drunken affair I guess

### February 2

The weather still grows warmer and the snow has entirely disappeared in the middle of the streetes. The ground is still white wherever I look beyond the town and the mountains look like a great immovable bank of clouds in the west.

Our band are getting to driving around town and playing a tune allmost every afternoon.

I can hear them somewhere as I write. Our street is getting to be a little quieter than it was from the fact that the dancehouse over the way is closed, and consequently there is not so much to draw a noisy crowd to the neighborhood.

There is still an occasional yell or shot however: force of habit I presume. Col. Moonlight is out in a letter to the legislature, warning them if they don't do something about these Indians, he will declare martial law

### February 3

Those bachalian soons of guns, "or some other feller", made the night hideous on this Street untill about two this morning, by firing pistols yells and howls.

I am inclined to think they are recruits for the 2nd Col: Cav, who are quartered above here somewhers

I am certain they are recruits for pandimonium any how

They can't be old soldiers or they would have more respect for a hospital than to take so much pains to disturb it's inmates. A train of coaches started for the states this morning under escort of about forty recruits for the 2nd.

Oh, pshaw! What's the use of leaving blank spaces like this? They look bad when one is looking over his diary.

### February 4

There is no doubt in my mind now, that the road is really dangerous down the river about three days travail, from what I can learn from those of the boys whom I have seene from the camp at Valley Station

They say there are parties of Indians to be seene every day in the neighborhood, of all sises, from six to a hundred and that they can get a skirmish allmost any day by riding back into the bluffs a few miles. The boys have come off best in every skirmish so far according to their own account, having killed several Indians without loosing a man except a few wounded

They have decidedly the advantage with their long range guns, for they can kill the red skinns and still keep out of reach

### February 5

Nothing unusual, nothing strange! Father Keeler made his usual call, and allso his usual prayer

Colorado is destined to have it's Indian war, and the Indians are destined to get cleaned out: but when the latter will be consumated is more than I am able to guess. Perhaps before another winter rolls around this territory may no longer belye her name, but be red color from the blood of her inhabitance. God forefend it!! What a name for a territory!

The Mexicans "couldn't see" the appropiateness of the name of Colorado volunteeres for *white* men, and so they called us Pike-us Peak-urs: and I dont know but it sound full as well

### February 6

Doctor Smith started for Fort Lyon today. Robinson and Cassidy left here after supper in an ambulance

Cassidy and Place[133] are going to Arrisona on some wild goose chase or other

They anticipate that there will be war between the United States and the French in Mexico, before many years, and think that by going down there and getting the "lay of the country", the "giberish", and politics, they will have a chance to make "an honest (?) penney or two" out of one party or the other. I wish the boys all sorts of good luck, but "can't see" any fortune in their undertaking.

### February 7

Another poor fellow has gone to his long home.

He was in the other Ward and I do not know his name, but he was a Mexican and has been here but a few days. He was burried this afternoon. I suppose his death was the effects of dissipation, and it's consequente prostration of sistem making it impossible for it to grapple with his disease

Which I believe was pulmonary but don't know

Col. Moonlight has declared martial law to take effect tomorrow, and has called for three hundred and sixty men for ninty days. I suppose our one horse legislature didn't come to time.

Go in Moonlight! your name's not sunshine, but "you'r on it"!!

### February 8

Weather warm. Verry little snow on the ground and none on the streets.

Another man died this morning. His name was George Vivian. I thought when I looked at him last night he would not live more than a couple of days, but I did not dream of his going so sudden. *he* was not in my ward either

I took a little exercise on horseback this afternoon for the first time in a dog's age, and came near getting my ribbs broken too. I was tightning the girth after having dismounted to adjust the saddleblanket when my horse becoming playfull. I let him have a little too much halter and he kicked me with all his power in my chest

### February 9

I took another little ride on Coxes[134] horse, but took care he didn't get another lick at my chest.

I went down the river about two miles and had a pleasant ride as far as the ride went, but the scenery was rather desolate and monotonous; the ground being covered with snow and the river with ice. There is no business allowed to be done here now except recruiting.

As maney can come into town as chose but none are allowed to go out without a pass. Even the wood and hay haulers have to get a pass to go home. Col. Moonlight says, "millitary law at *best* is arbitrary", and I guess some of the cittizins of Colorado will begin to think themselves no better than soldiers after awhile.

*February 10*

I went up cherry creek and across to the burriingground, which is considerable of a citty of itself notwithstanding the healthiness of the country. Among the names upon the toombstones and head-boards, I recognised several who had been shot one time and another in this town

Possibly one third of those graves are filled by those who have died by violent hands. I stopped and had a chat for an hour with the thre men who were digging a grave. One of them has lived with the Indians a good deal, and he seeing I am a soldier, gave me some information about their mode of warfare, signs etc, which may be of use to me sometime

*February 11*

What good is there in keeping a diary, unless you can write down something every day which will be of use to you or someboddy else at some future time!

"Learn something every day" says the old spelling book.

Now I believe I *do* learn something, if not *every* day, *nearly* every day: And it would seeme that the use of a diary would be to jot down these little items of knowledge, to assist memory in their retention for future use; but this knowledge often comes to me in such a form as to make it impossable for me to put it into words: and too, 'it is often' of such a character that I care not to retain it. Still I consider it of little use to keep a record of unimportant incidents. Yet I have nothing else

*February 12*

Every thing all right!

I went through my usual duties and took my usual ride on horseback, but not untill after supper this time. My room is still full of patients. As fast as they get well and go away their places are filled by others

Sometimes there are from one to four vacant beds but they are soon filled. There are the wounded from the hospital at Ft Lyon who are sent here as soon as they are able to take the trip. These with the new recruits, who are constantly getting sick, and Q, M'r's men, and accasionally a destitute cittizen, keep the hospital full an allow us no rest.

### February 13

I was deprived of my usual ride today because some of the other boys had been riding the horse, and I do not like to ride a tired animal. More new patients. We have two of the new territorial ninty day men allready in the hospital, before their names were barely dry on the enlistment papers. All I ask is that they dont *all* of them serve their time out here on *our* hands. This evenings paper brings us the news that the tellegraph is all right, Gen. Curtis is remove, two thousand troops are enroute for the protection of the platt route, etc, etc, all of which is good.

Frank Holms[135] came in today. He has a story to tell of an escape himself and two others made, which would fill 6 pages like this.

### February 14

We have men here who have been in nearley every part of the united states and territories, and as is natural nearley every one has something to tell of his personal experiances in one part of the country or other, which are more or less interesting, of course. The most of these anecdotes are too long to undertake to transcribe uppon a page of this size. One fellow, Linpson,[136] an old regular, has a rich fund of personal experiances, of life in the regular armey before the war, and since, in Arrisonia, New Mexico, Kansas and Missouri. He was in Quantrell's camp three days before the destruction of Laurance,[137] and afterwards as a spy in two other camps of rebel gurelles on the border

### February 15

Men usually work for money or some other object. A soldier will work at any thing out of the usual line of a soldiers duty, provided there is some inducement to do so; but generally not without. Now I as just like other men I want some inducement to do so or I am not satisfied to do more than the comon duty of a soldier.

I am willing to do, and intend to do my duty as well as I know how wherever I may happen to be placed: but I did not enlist for a hospital attendant, and as there is no extra pay or other inducement to keep me here, except (as some might think) cowardice, I shall ask to be relieved as soon as there is any show for active service in the company

*February 16*

A light snow fell during the night making everything look wintery again.

Two of our convalescents reported for duty this morning or rather one convalecent and one hypocondriac or bumer: for in my opinion he is no better today than when he came here, and he was just as well when he come here as he ever was in his life

I've got my own opinion of such fellows! I am as liable to be mistaken as any body, and in this case I may have mentaly done a fellow being an injustice: for it is hard to tell whether a man is really sick or not, sometimes, unless you take their word for it. Two new patients from down among the Indians, this evening.

*February 17*

Snow nearly gone again. Streets muddy. Considerable stirring about on the streetes.

A Co. of the denver malitia have had their quartirs a few doors below us; and there has been a continual galloping back and forth here ever since they drew their horses

They have a pretty good lott of horses. They expect to leave today. The two new patients are a couple of cittizens who were wounded by the Indians in the neighborhood of Valley station some time ago. One has lost his right arm, and the other has an awfull hole in his skull which lays bare about a square inch of his brane.

Did'n't get any exercise on horseback today

*February 18*

Rather warm, and quite pleasent. Two Co's. from the mountains came in this afternoon. George Lowe[138] is Cl. G. of one of them, and Bud. is private in one

Good news from the states by tellegraph this evening. Other things as usual.

I do wish I would get a letter from someboddy or other I haven't had one from hom for nearley six weeks and allthough I am satisfied they have been written, it is poor consolation unless I can receive them. I have not written lately, but, What's the use to write when there is no mails! I expect the mail will soon comence running again and I guess I shall have to write up a batch against they do

*February 19*

It takes me 'till twelve now to get through dressing the wounds in my ward.

There is one leg, two thighs three arms, one hedd, and two backs, which I have to dress every morning and most of them again every evening. Father Keeler paid his visit.

I contrived to get time to go to church this evening, by dressing some of the wounds before, and some after I went. I heard Mr. Day deliver his fare-well address, which was I think the best sermon I ever heard him preach. And I allways liked to hear him. He used to preach in the same room which I now ocupy.

He is young, rather elequont, and apparantly cincere. At least he is earnest.

*February 20*

A beautifull sheat of snow fell during the night, to the depth of about three inches, and every thing consequently looks a little more wintery again. Each day brings it's duties and it's burdons and each is so much like the other that it is impossible to distingu one from the other, to tell a sunday from a week day. It is this that makes time seem long while it is passing, and short afterwards

One can look back upon the spaces of time when every day was like the other, and allthough they were relatively long, they look like mere specs. While other spaces, 'though short, were croweded with incidents, and seeme long

*February 21*

It is said that we are the workeres out of our own fortunes. Is this wholey so! Is there not an inmmutable inchangable fate, destiny connected with our lives over which we have so little controll, as to be no more than semifree agents? If this is not so, why do we drift about through life which-ever way the tide of circumstances carry us? I believe no one is born into the world mearley to fill up; as some captains sometimes enlist a recruit whom they know to be unfit for a soldier, but to *do* something which will be for the advancement of the right. And he who fullfills not his part, had better never been borne. What am I for??

*February 22*

Washington's birthday! I remember that one year ago the boys at Ft.

Lyon being dissatisfied becaus the officers did not make some kind of a demonstration in honor of the day, got up an immence horse fiddle and went around by their quarters and groaned them with it 'till they were glad to treat.

After which we rigged a four horse team and filled the waggon up with the best singers, and drove it, accompanied by outriders, around, and gave them a serrinade. They came down so heavy at this that We all got "on it" before we were done

### February 23

Weather moderately cool, but warm for winter. I don't know as I have done or seene anything very strange or extreordinary to day, or worth recording. I have mearly done my usual duties. Performed my everyday routine, with my usual amount of perplexities and grumblings. Though as to the grumblings, I believe I am getting less and less impatience at little perplexities as I grow older, or as I am placed in possitions where they are apt to multiply. I begin to think this hospital disciplin will be a benefit to me after all

### February 24

An education! An education! Oh, why was I not borne rich so that I might have been educated! Simply that I was borne poor so that I might be educated!

Book knowledge is a great thing! and I would that I had a thousand times as much as I have not.

But supposening I had what good would it do? Why, I might make myself rich by it's use. Yes, but to make myself rich, has a verry narrow contracted object. If I could do no better than that with knowledge, I would deserve not to have it. Anyhow I guess what little I do know will be enough to serve *my selfish* ends, and what's the use of grumbling.

### February 25

Weather moderate and in fact a little muddy in the streetes. The hospital gets along about as usual; convalescents being sent away, and new sick and wounded filling their places: if it goes on in this way for a month or two longer there will have to be built another hospital to hold the patients. If some one had told me three months ago that I had the patience to dress as many wounds as I am now doing every day, I should have thought they knew nothing about me and were poor judges of character. Well, it is not a verry nice job, I must say! But somebody has got to *do it*.

### February 26

Inspire me, Oh sence! While I write a page. Look down on me this once, Be thou or clown or sage.

For there is not a doubt, But you can help to fill It up, by merely looking out For any little thing that will Be foolishness ness or nonscence Or if you should happen to hit On something that would be scence Just till it me right quick For I am at the present Most sorely tried in my own mind about what to say for myself, as There has nothing of any particular note happened to me or in my neighborhood, and I am a verry poor hand to write of things in the abstract. I can talk much better than than I can write. There if This page a'int full, What is the use of trying to fill it?

### February 27

This evening the citty was illuminated in honor of the fall of Charlestown, and every body as promanading the streetes. The doctor and his wife with two other ladies, and two other gentlemen, came in and paid the patients all a visite this evening. This appeared to enliven the boys up considerably, and I have no doubt has done them a good deal of good. Denver is out in fine stile; every window in the place nearley is lit up with as many candels as there are panes of glass. Transparancies with names of favorite generals, or sentances, poretratts of old Abe, and Others, etc, etc.

### February 28

We were mustered by his most scerene and unasuming mightiness, Col. Moonlight. He is about six feet in his boots, rather spare, broad shouldered and straight: long thin nose, small chin which is cleanshaven: heavy check whiskers and mustaches which cover the most of his face: rather high fore head clear eye, (disremember the color) but not verry large head. There is wanting the usual tincel and glitter of the regular officer, as the usual hautier allso; but gentelmanly maners suply the place of both. On the whole I like his appearance.

### March 1

A little cloudy and some snow: rather cold, but not windy. We have lately been getting a small library of forty volumes for the benefit of the convalescents. There are two or three of travails, Cooks voyiges, some poetry, etc, etc; some of them are pretty good books, and some are indifferent: They are "a nice thing" for a hospital anyhow Dr. Hamilton got hold of them somehow. They belong I believe to the Sanitary Commission. I can generally manage to get about two hours to read during the day, and I mean to improve it as well as I can while I stay here

### March 2

There is one thing, a hospital nurse will make for all this hard work which will partially repay him for his wear and tear of patience and constitistion, if he does his duty, and that is a great many friends: which is no small thing after all, when it is looked at in the proper light, and I don't know but will repay me for the little time I have spent here with out other (and more substantial as the world goes) remuneration. But whether this will be enough of an inducement to keep me here the ballance of my time, I verry much doubt! There are no other but philanthropic motives for staying here.

### March 3

I don't know as I have got anything particular to say for myself to night, but I suppose I shall have to fill this page with some bolderdash or other to keep up appearances if for nothing more. This is, in my opinion, not a propper mode of filling up a diary; for a diary should not hav anything in it, but what was written under the free untrameled impulse of the moment.

That which is written merely to fill up a page can have verry little interest, be of verry little benefit.

### March 4

I suppose that honest old Abe will go through the serrimony of inaugeration again today. I should like to be present and hear from his own lips what he will have to say. But us Pike's Peakers, will have to be content to wait a few weeks before we can even *read* what has transpired at the capital this day.

We get a semioccasional tellegram, which informs us of the move-ments of our armies, whenever there is a move, provided the newsmongers can find out any thing about it themselves. But all this is nothing about what I have done today! Well! I have done my duty!

### March 5

Well! I'll be darned if I dont begin to think it is a little doubtfull whether

I make out to fill this diary, without having some blank pages in it; especially if I stay here. Here are a couple of pages which have been left blank for four days, and now I must come back and fill them up somehow or other I suppose.

I'm an odd sort of a genious, myself, if I am to believe what they all say. Among other characteristics, I am a noted grumbler!

Yet I cannot remember to have grumbled at any real service or unavoidable hardship since I have been a soldier. Nevertheless some of the boys, and most of the officers in the Co. call me a grumbler. I know, that I am addicted to talking, more perhaps than is good for me: and that if I have anything to say about anything which I think is not right, I am apt to express myself in pretty strong terms, regardles of who may happen to be with in ear-shot or present.

This of course does not make me friends verry fast among a certain class, and I suppose it is foolish for me to do so. They say it is! But I cant *help* it for it is my nature, and I am not yet convinced it is wrong.

### March 7

This has been a rather cold day, and somewhat cloudy. Played a game of freeze out poker for a jack-nife this evening and got beat of course. Never did know how to play and never expect to. Might have known I could'n't Win. I did not speak of that becaus it is the only thing out of the common run.

The fact of the business is, I have been as bussy as I could be all day, and did not get time to play the game without interruptions. High, Oh! Well! when I'm bust I hain't got much time to grumble, have I?

### March 8

It was pretty cold this morning, and indeed half the night. I did'n't sleep Warm enough. It thawed a little this afternoon however

Poker is getting to be quite fashionable among some of our convalescents nowadays. There is one or two games running the most of the time in my room. don't see any prospect of anything like a rest or relaxation even, for me; for instead of having any easier times when my patients get well; they are sent away and others come who are more helpless than the old ones ever were, aparantly.

### March 9

A large government train came in this morning, accompanied by a considerable number of cittizins trains, making in all about 250 Waggons. Ed. Tuttle come in to see us this afternoon, having come in with the train. He says they "have not seene an Indian!" Probably their large number had more to do with their seeing no Indians than any other caus.

The ground froze hard last night, and it has continued cold all day.

Several teamsters of the big train came in to have their fingers dressed, having froze them down below

### *March 10*

Oh! Why dont I get at least one letter?

I have been waiting long and not impatiently for the mails to resume running, and now they have been running for over two weeks, but still I get no letters. I cannot wait as patiently now I know the mails are all right. Verry good news by Tellegraph this evening. I "cant see" how rebelldom is going to hold out much longer.

Weather a little warmer, business more brisk or at least more people stirring about! Probably on account of the train comeing in yesterday.

### *March 11*

Still warmer! I took a walk uptown this afternoon for the first time in nearly two weeks. I found cherry creek running to the depth of about eight inches. There is a stream about four inches deep and six feet wide running down this street. I found things in the citty looking about as usual, the gambling saloons running and business apparantly as brisk as usual.

I am beginning to hope, just a little, that this will be the last year of the war

### *March 12*

And still warmer!

The rill down the street continues to be about the same size, but cherrycreek has increased to a river, and will take a horse to the saddle skirts.

Father Keeler is beginning to neglect us I fear, for this is the second or third Sunday since he has given us a call. Perhaps *we* are more to be blamed for this than he, for we have never paid a great deal of attention or took much interest in him, or rather his prayers. Still I never saw any one show anything but respect to him, at any time, allthough no great amount of interest was shown.

*March 13*

Dark and cloudy with a light snow at three P.M. which gradually increased to a storm at sundown. Wet, sloppy and disagreeable on the streetes. There is something eminantly suggestive in this gloom. Without it we should never be able to appreciate the bright joyous sunshine; of which (sunshine not gloom) we have if anything to great a preponderance in this country.

It typafies one phase of the human mind as the sunshine does another. Each, also suggests different phases of society

*March 14*

Cold, Wet, nasty! With mild, spasmodic attempts to snow, which has at last been crowned with success at five.

Notwithstanding the disagreeableness of the Weather, the street has been all day unusually busy with men on foot, on horseback, in buggies and waggons, going to or returning from town; or rather the more busy part of it: namely Blake, F, and Larimer streetes

Denver surely is a busy place whether in sunshine or the shaadow of a storm of clouds.

Business does not mind, cold or wet, mud or snow, here.

*March 15*

Ground white, sun bright, weather cool this morning.

I had commenced to write a little on this page but was interupted, and now come back after nearly a month to fill it up if I can. I have now had a little experience in a hospital and know that an attendant has no "soft snap" or "good thing" at all: as some are foolish enough to think, but the rather has more to do and worse than in any other branch of the servace. And also that he is the poorest paid according to what is expected of him, of any man in the servace. His pay is in the heartfelt thanks of his patients, seldom spoken but as seldom wanting, and with this he must be content

*March 16*

I don't know as I ever found a better place to study the human character than here. When a man is sick he is pretty apt to show his disposition planely.

I presume there are a great many who die in hospitals for the want of a little pure grit.

When a man gets verry sick it is a hard matter to bring him up unless he can be got to think he will get well. Hope is the best medicin! I have to resort to all plans to bring some of the dispondant ones to cherefullness. Some I talk to as I would to a child, some I joke, and some I have to scold to make them angry.

I believe it to be my duty

### March 17

I am in hopes the Paymaster will pay us off before long, and when he does I mean to get relieved from duty here. I don't believe it is healty for me to stay here, and I must try and get out of doors again. My health does not get verry good and I am as pale as any patient here.

The Paymaster, Major Crawford, has been here three or four days sick with the rheumatism and I don't know as he will be able to pay aney body off verry soon, but I hope so. I presume he will pay us hospital boys off as soon as he is able to do so.

### March 18

I wish I could get out of doors more! Here I am from daylight 'till midnigth bussy as I can be all the time going up and down, up and down the room, giving solutions and powders, dressing a wound here or adjusting a blanket or pillow there, with all these eyes watching every move I make; every look, or gesture, word or tone, is weighed by fevered braines, and probably has it's weight, for better or worse. The responsibillity wears on me, as well as the labor and vitiated atmosphere. I *must* get away from here, and yet, I would like to see all these poor fellows convalesant first.

The ladies of denver seeme to have no knowledge of the suffering in their midst or they surely would come and visite the hospital once in a while. 'Twould do more good than all the medicins & bandages in the dispensary. Mrs. Hamilton comes once in a while & it seemes to do the boys a deal of good

### March 19

This morning I was standing at the front door having an arguement about the killing of women and children of Indians, and I was expressing myself in pretty strong terms when the steward came to the door and checking me ordered me to "dry up" or something to the same effect: by which I felt insulted, and I told him he had no business to dictate how I was to talk, nor what I was to talk about

He said he had a right and I must stop it! I told him he had no right to give orders in that respect and I would not stand it. That I was not obliged to stay here, and I would leave. Accordingly I asked the Doctor to be relieved, and he said he would see about tomorrow

### March 20

I asked the Doctor again to be relieved!

He tried to get me to agree to stay, but as I would not do it he fineally said he would relieve me today! Accordingly he sent me an order relieving from duty and ordering me to report to Capt' Soule[139]

I went to Soules office but it was So late that it was shut up, so I will have to sleep here tonight!

The doctor says I have done better than anybody else he could get, and wants me to stay two or three days longer. He admits however that it is my right to be relieved whenever I ask it

### March 21

Went to Soule's office and he told me to come again at noon.

Went again at noon and Soule went to Dr. Hamillton and told him the Ad'g't Gen'l told him to ask him why he ordered this man to report to him (Soule). Hamilton said he would see about it, and started for the Ag't's office. I waited half an hour and as he didn't come back, I went to dinner. After dinner I hunted up the Dr and he told me to report to the Adg't Gen'l. I did so and he ordered me to repot to Lieut' Willson.[140]

He ordered me to repot to Seargent Turner[141] and he showed me a tent where I could sleep

### March 24

Been laying in the tent the biggest share of the day. I wrote a couple of letters, and received one

Went down town this evening and bummed around the gambling saloons a couple of hours. Won nothing, and lost nothing but my time.

### March 25

The Orderly Seargent ordered me to report to Lieutenant Olney[142] this morning, and I did so: he told me to be ready to march monday morning. I have been at the hospital nearly all day making myself a chest and waiting to be paid off as Maj. Crawford promised me he would do after a detachment of A Co were all paid. He paid the Provost' guard, the band and a detachment at Camp weld before he got around to me, which he did about eight Oclock in the evening. I received four months pay and an installment of bounty, and fifteen dollars Clothing money

### March 26

The boys have put up a gambling tent with tables and seats in camp and the game of montee has been running pretty high all day. Some have got broke and some have of course won considerable. One fellow lost all he had which was $150.00 dealing: another dealer lost $85.00, another $65.00. One fellow had nothing this morning but two decks of cards which he sold for $5.00, and he won about $130.00 with it: One fellow borrowed $0.50, and won $85.00 with it etc, etc, that's the way the money goes. The fellow who put up the tent, and sells cigarrs and beer, collects the table rents, etc, Makes more than any of them

### March 27

I huseled around and got my trapps togather and took them to H Co. camp and loaded them into a waggon in readiness to start which we did about two Oclock. They gave me a horse to ride and after going down to Adg't's office for the Co. F letters, I followed on after the command. We came five miles up the platt and camped at a house and correll kept here by young Fisher

The weather is fine but the roads are muddy. Every one thinks it a wonder it don't storm as it usually does when a command leaves denver.

### March 28

I woke up this morning under about 8 inches of snow. I was warm and comfortable and hated to get out of bed into the cold snow, but fineally made the raise. I found my pants wet and covered with snow, my jacket the same, and my boots the same. The boots I could'n't get on and I nearly froze my fingers getting dressed.

The Lieutenant concluded he would not leave here today, but I guess he meant us instead of himself, for he saddled up about ten and started for town. We have spent a most uncomfortable day

### March 29

The sun came out today, but we have remained in camp as the Lieu't' thought the roads would be too bad to travail

The sun has shown so glarringly all day uppon the snow as to allmost blind one. My eyes feele the effects of it and a bad cold combined pretty severly. The boys have been as bussy as they could be gambling all day in the house. I got into a small mess of five besides myself today and I guess I shall have a better chance to live than in the Co. mess as that is not carried on any better than other Co. messes are

### March 30

We pulled out half an hour after sunrise this morning and reached Richisen's about twelve oclock. It was pretty cold riding till about ten, and the sun on the snow has been pretty bad on my eyes.

Our mess waggons were not more than an hour and a half behind us, and as we had got some wood and built a fire, we soon had our coffee bread and bacon ready for dinner

We had selected a dry place for our mess fire but it was a good ways from the waggons and up hill at that: which made it rather a hard job to carry the mess kit to it.

The boys say they are going over the range with the fire next time

### March 31

Got on the road by the time the sun got over the hills. As we were so far out of camp with our cooking opperations we came near being too late to get our kit into the waggon. One of the boys got up so late that he came for his breakfast just as the waggons were starting and we were packing up. T'was hard for a man to go without his breakfast, but it would'nt do to have our kit left behind: so he had to loose it! He cursed a little becaus he "was'nt waked sooner", but there was no help for it. We camped about one and a half miles beyond the Widdow Coberlies, and about a dozzen of us went into the house and got a square meal

### April 1

Again we got a pretty early start! I let Jim Hill ride my horse and I rode in a waggon. I happened to get into a waggon driven by a mexican and I bothered him all day asking him the meaning of words, and the names of things. As he cannot speak a word of english, and I but a little spanish it was rather a tegious job trying to talk. There are two mexican teamsters in the train, and they can neither of them talk english, nor can the waggonmaster, or any of the other teamsters speak a word of spanish. We did not stop at the dirty woman's ranche, but came six miles farther and camped on mud creek. A pleasant place to camp! No snow!

### April 2

Three men—who were all recruits within a few months, deserted last night, or rather this morning, for one of them went on guard at one oclock. 

A detail of a seargent and three men were sent after them. The Lieutenant wanted to know which way they had gone? Some thought one way, and some another: but none knew. I told him I thought to mexico, for I had noticed two of them talking verry privately togather, day before yesterday, and Polanger soon came to me and asked me verry particularly about Taos and how to go there. The detail took the road towards mexico. We reached Colorado Citty about ten oclock, Where we have camped. We have heard of the deserters, and the detail three hours behind them

### April 3

Were on the march at sun rise, and have come to Young's ranche, a good thirty miles.

Am tireder this evening than at any other time on the trip

We got here about one oclock and as our mess waggons were close behind us, we soon had some coffee and bacon cooked for dinner, which helped to rest us better than anything else could.

### April 4

We came [to] the cutoff[143] where we experianced another snowstorm on the divide. Arrived at Boonville about noon and I found Co F camped close by in log houses. Nearley all of the Vet's of old Co. F. are here and I am glad I have got amongst them once more. I soon had the offer of a bunk in two different cabbins, but as I could'n't ocupy both, I had to put up with one.

I am now domiciled with Sam Lanis, Jime Boies, John Webber, and Frazier.[144] The camp is built in the form of a triangle, with some large cottenwoods in the middle. A line of cabbins on the south side, one on the west, and the stables on the north

### April 5

Considerable snow fell during the night, and the Co. which I came down with have remained here all day. I have got a good place to board, at Johnson's. There are seven of us who board there

We have been playing freezeout for a pair of bootes, and have played about a dozzen games. I got stuck three times and won two. The river runs close along by the south line of cabbins and there is good fishing ground all along some one or other is continually fishing when it is not too windy. The fish are mostly small, but there is once in a while a kind of shad caught of two or three pounds weight.

Cat fish of from ½ lb to 2 lbs are common.

### April 6

Have been laying in the cabbin all day with nothing to do, which is not verry hard on me at present: rather fatiguing to be sure, but still I can stand it

Wrote a letter to my Mother. Co H boys left for Ft Lyon this morning.

I found little Jim who belongs to Jim Hill, running around the camp cold wet and hungry this evening. He was as tickled a fellow as ever was to see me, and so I took him under my special care untill I see his owner again. Jim Hill would'nt take considerable money for him.

### April 7

Am on guard today for the first time in eleven months or more. It is just eleven months since I left the Co. to go to the states on furlough

The weather has been rather cold all day, so as to make a coat comfortable. There is but two posts, one at the guardhouse, and one at the quartermaster's corelle over a pile of corn. I am number one first relief and my orders are to let no man take his horse out sadled without a pass: allow none to turn their horses loose; none to feede either hay or corn except at stable call: and to keepe all loose cattle out of the square

### April 8

I was on stable polise today and had to work half a day. Our camp is located in the only wet place in the neighborhood as usual. It is a courious fact that nearly every post or camp which is located in this country is invariably on a lower piece of ground than that around it, and consequently is wet when there is any wet at all.

Every thing is so dry here, the greater portion of the year, that the probability of a wet time is seldom thought of in the location of camps. The lower places are prettier in the summer, and it is more natural to camp upon them

### April 9

And this is sunday! We had co. inspection this morning as of old

As I have often remarked before, there is little difference betweene a sunday and a weekday with the Trooper.

Little or no atention or respect is paid to it in the servace. Of battles fought, or expiditions undertaken, I guess as maney have been on sunday as on any other day of the week

We have no chaplain and consequently no kind of public worship: unless the weekly inspection might be called so, for it comes about as near being a farce as any public worship I ever witnessed

### April 10

Myself, Killmore and Piles, crossed the river in the skiff and went about a mile back on the bottom to a kind of dead pond or slough fishing. We had verry bad luck! Only one bite betweene the three of us! Piles caught a cat of about one pound weight. A pretty good day for fishing too! There are broad firtile bottoms here, and to judge by appearances, there was a good deele of hay cut here last fall. The grass is beginning to start. If the horses were driven across the river they would do verry well pretty soon

### April 15

We have received pretty authentic reports that the denver papers have the news that General Lee with his whole armey has been captured. All appear well pleased, and believe the news: but there is no noise made about it, or any great demonstations of joy manifested.

Every body seemes to think it a matter of course, a foregone conclusion, long talked of, expected, and understood; therefore calling for no particular demonstration now, allthough all seeme glad to know that everything works so well, as all felt confident things would. What next!

### April 16

Warm and pleasant

There is considerable talk of the speedy close of the war, and our discharge! Variou conflicting opinions are advanced, some contending that we will be discharged by the fourth of July, and others holding that were peace declared now, we would not be released before January. It is reported in camp that there are men in denver who are willing to bet any amount— allmost that peace is declared now.

D. K. Baily[145] came up from Ft Bent this evening, and I had to enlarge the bunk for his accomodation

### April 17

The boys have some of them been at work putting up a swing, uppon the limb of one of these large cottonwoods in camp. Someone or other is continually swinging on it, and, I expect not many days will pass, before some unlucky 'cus will get his neck broke, or his leg, or arm, or possably his head may come in such close proximity to the ground that he will not only see stars, but feele them; and if he escapes with that, will 'thank his stars', that worlds did not appear and disappear instead.

Freezeoute is the game! Three pairs of pants ahead am I, and but two shirts behind! As long as I can keep even I can play, unless some other passtime I can find

### April 18

And once more I am on guard! This time I am number two third relief, and my post is the correll to guard a pile of corn from a lot of horses, raw boned and poore, cavalyard stock: and also to keep morso thieving men from taking that which not to him belongs. For who knows what temptations might or might not beset some poore deluded soldier or citizin, to take of this corn small or large amounts, and self appropriate it; 'though knowing it to be our general uncles property. While, under guard of armed Trooper, some will ever think of such a thing as purloining even the smallest quantity.

### April 20

This is my regular day for stable police duty, but I was ordered to go for a load of wood across the river with two others, for the bake house, which is run by Alex. Cochran and Alex. Monarque[146] of the old Company, and that is all the work I have had this day to do.

Corporal McGahey[147] came and told me to be ready in half an hour to go for hay this afternoon, and I was ready but no one said hay to me again, and I noticed about an hour afterwards that the hay had been hauled without my help somehow. Verry Windy but not extryordinarily cold

### April 22

Today every man was called out to police the camp, and it took us 'till noon to get through. Every man had to be on hand, some with willow brooms some with shovels, some with pitch forks, and one with a rake. The whole camp was pitched, shoveled and swept as clean as possible and the dirt hauled off.

I got Bill Meencer's[148] fishpole and line and fished about two hours, I caught one fish about five inches long, and had one bite besides: got my hook fast, and worked half an hour to get it loose: got my feet wet, and my patience tried, and then quit.

### April 24

Here is about a sinopsis of a day's work for me when not on duty.

I get up a little after sunrise the most of the time, and go to rollcall or sometimes am too late, and get marked absent I presume; After rollcall I go over to Johnstons and eat a pretty good breakfast for a soldier; I then come back to the cabbin, and take a smoke, lounge in the cabbin, or about camp, take two or three more smokes, go to dinner, take another smoke, lounge about camp, or go fishing if it a'int too windy, smoke two or three times, go to rollcall at five and then to supper: after supper I smoke of course, talk and lounge 'till bed time

### April 25

On guard again over the same pile of corn, with the same horse and same men to watch, under the same orders. It is a verry easy thing to stand guard once in five or six days, but as it is the onley duty we have to do, it is considered a kind of hardship, and a great many will allways try to get out of it as often as they can. All kinds of excuses to get on the sick report are sometimes made. There is none or verry little of this here however becaus it is lauaghed down

Nobody likes to "play the sick report" and have to take medicin, and be laughed at too if he can avoid it

The weather is begining to get somewhat warm in the middle of the day.

### April 26

Since I was relieved from guard at nine oclock this morning, I did nothing untill after dinner when I lay down to take a nap and slep all afternoon missing the rollcall at five and comeing near getting in the guardhouse in consequense. I slept so much and so strong that I am as dumb as a doore nail, or a watter soaked log. I feele as neare like a nonenity as it is within my comprehention to know what that is. Whether I am myself or somebody elses self, I don't know

### April 27

I had to help police the stables, this morning, and haul the hay this afternoon. Have lounged about the cabbin, took my usual number of smokes, for the balance of my day's work. Mail came in about noon; got a letter from home, and answered it. There were a batch of orders read at rollcall this evening, all about some General or some other Gen'l assuming command of the department of the planes, and some Brevett General of the sub district of the south and west H'd Qr's at Denver, Saluting officers, wearing the uniform, transfeering or reenlisting in an engineere regt, and lot of other millitary bosh

### April 28

The millitary disciplin is begining to get more close and irksome. It wont do now to appear at roocall without a full suit of uniform. I have no jacket with the stripes on, and I expect every day when the Lieutenant will order me to draw one. Untill I get special orders to do so, I shall not draw one as I have two jackets now.

### April 29

I am detailed to go below with some of the boys, for something or other I don't know what.

I ai'nt particular where I am sent or what it is for, but I would like to have a horse to ride.

This being dismounted cavalry is'nt verry pleasant

If I had that old rawboned Texas-Apachee horse I sold a year ago, now, I would be all right, and feele like myself again.

I don't feele like more than half of myself without a horse. It seemes as if the best half of me is gone, and the half that is left is a verry poor excuse for a man, or a soldier.

### April 30

I couldn't escape the weekly inspection allthough detached and supposed to be away from the Co. We got our traps into a waggon and left camp about three oclock, and come three or four miles down the river, to the camp of the hay train. there are fifteene of us. Onley one noncom in the party, and only three mounted men

There is a canoe here, and as the train is going below a couple of us have made paddles, with the intention of running it down the river. This seemes kind of old fassioned and home like. I like it!

## *May 1*

This morning Tubby Harpham[149] and I got into an old log canoe, which the teamsters had here, and which they had no more use for, and started to run it down the river, thinking we could probably reach spring bottom by noon.

We got along verry well the first ten or fiftene miles, allthough we found the river verry crooked.

After that we began to encounter sand barrs, which became more numerous as we proceeded down, and we had considerable wading to do. Our progress got slower and slower and we began to dispair of reaching spring bottom at all. At last just before sundown we tied up our boat, at a place where the river took another backward sweep, and came on afoot, and reached here about dark.

## *May 2*

We went up and got our canoe, which we found only about four miles by a straight line from camp, and run it down. 'Tis nearley ten miles by the river. We found the river had raised a little during the night and our canoe was less trouble to us than before

I dont think I have aney verry particular desire however to navigate this river in a log canoe for a living. It may be all verry nice to "float down the river in a little log canoe, but I 'ca'nt see it', when the river is no higher than it is now. This is a tolerable pleasant place for a soldier to be stationed at, but it is rather lonesome

## *May 3*

There is an empty cabbin here which we have appropriated for a cookhouse, and another which the station keeper uses for a corn, and lumberroom which we have appropriated as a sleepingroom. this latter is in fact one of the double cabbins of which the house is composed There is an open, covered space betweene, and some of the boys made their beds in there

Frazier and I have put our blankets togather, and made our bed out of doors; and a "poor old" bed it is: only thirteene blankets betweene us, and two single bedticks. It's a wonder we don't freeze. The first winter I was a soldier, I had but two verry poor blankets all winter.

*May 4*

Frazier and I concluded to move our blankets into the porch, or open space betweene the cabbins of the stationhouse, as there came up a rainstorm this afternoon, and we had carried our blankets in there.

The boys now all have a roof to sleepe under. Three sleepe in our cookhouse, Three in the station keepers milkhouse, which is under, and dug into the hill, three in the porch, and the ballance in the cornhouse. I do'nt know what the station keeper thinks of our taking such unlimited possesion of his premises, nor do I care. we are here for the protection of the station and we have no tents.

*May 6*

This morning after breakfast, Frazier and myself "went on cook", for five days.

Of all the duties of a soldier, cooking is the one I like the least to do: and it is one, of which, I think I have done about as much as the majority if not a little more, untill within about eighteene months back. Ther is no use of a fellow grumbling about having to cook, for it has got to be done, and you may as well do it as anybody. Still it is a disagreeable job. Grumbling however will only make it the more so. Therefore he who grumbles at it is a fool!

*May 7*

The train which camped here last night, was gone and our own breakfast over before I awoke.

Nearley all hands pitched out after breakfast, and gathered a fine lot of greenes for dinner. We gathered lambsquarters. The river is raising again and has backed the water up a slough to the house: about eighty rods

*May 10*

A couple of the boys took a couple of the horses and went after a beefe this morning. They came in with one about two hours before dark and we butchered him and threw everything but the meat into the river

It is not verry fat but it is better than old bacon that I know of. The weather continues cold. Snow fell a little this forenoon and it is rather dark and cloudy.

Four Mexicans came along just at night on foot from Fort Lyon, and have camped here

A horseman from the other direction is also stopping here tonight

## *May 11*

The sun came out bright and clear, and the weather is a little warmer. The boys feele a little better now we have pleanty of beefe. We cooked our last meal this morning and are now relieved.

A man from up the river stopped here for the night, who tried to convince us that this is wednesday, but could'nt come it, and fineally had to acknowledge that he had lost a day. The coach is due but has not come in yet, Talking about the coach brought on the argument of the day of the week. River raised about two inches today: it is now verry near full banks, and runns over the bottoms into the sloughs in one or two places

## *May 12*

Coach came and went during the night; there was but one letter for our outfitt: none for me but All. Randall[150] and some of the boys from denver came in, on their way to Fort Lyon, and they brought me one.

These boys all have some big stories to tell about Gen'l Guy Henry, and his abuse of the rank he holds, in Denver. I am sure I would not wish to hold his office, and be thought of by the men, as he is. Some of the best soldiers, and most quiet honest men, he has just under arrest, in order to show his authority. Instead of intimidaing, this onley has an tendancy to exasperate the boys to disobedience

## *May 13*

The coach came in and went out again last night about twelve oclock, as much as twelve hours ahead of time

I neglected to write write letters yesterday, and now it is too late for this mail. All Brondale took little Jimmie with him this morning. I had become attatched to him, and hated to part with him, but he did not belong to me, and I had no right to keep him from his master.

'Ti's cloudy this morning and coole. River an inch lower this morning

## *May 14*

"All quiet at" camp sowbelley! Pleasant weather and warm. Meusketoes begin to show themselves, but not in verry anoying quantities. Out of tobacco; which has nearly the same meaning as, out of heart. Grass growes fineally! some places it is six or eight inches high. Cottonwoods now in full leaf, and the river slowly on the decline. Conversation lively, but no news. Wanted! Something to pass away the time.

Fish wo'nt bite, Antelope keep distant, rabbits verry scarce, but still pleanty of first rate country to hunt in.

### May 15

The river remains at about the same stage, if anything a little lower. Still warm but not sultrey. If we had any way to get the news of the world, our time would not hang so heavely on our hands. As it is, with verry little reading matter, and that of the poorest trashiest kind, principally, and no other resourse but such as ixists in our own minds, for amusement or passtime, with such restless fond of excitement, men as ourselves, it is a wonder how we contrive to content ourselves as well as we do.

All are looking forward to the time of their discharge with a restless, not to be satisfied inpatience, eager for news, ready to believe anything good, and anxious for the end.

### May 16

We have had a little company today. Mr. Searse came up from below, and he said there was a lot of Mexicans about ten miles below who tried to make him think they were Indians, and in fact he did think so, but by reckenoitering he found out his mistake. They were naked, with breechclothes and blankets, some on one side of the river, and some on the other, and they were dancing around and having a regular Indian powwow, whooping and yelling.

A couple more of the boys came along this evening on their way from Denver to fort Lyon. They speak better of Guy Henry than any of the others.

### May 17

Some of the boys went into the timber and cut a lot of house logs this morning. It is our intention to have a house of our own. The river continues to rise and [the] slough back of the house has become quite a lake. Our skiff is kept in use during the coole of the morning and evening by someone or other of the boys paddleing about in it.

We have verry little actual use for it, but it serves to pass away some of our extra time of which we have so much, and we should feele sadley its loss now we have becaome used to having it. The Co. team came down this evening

### May 18

We went to work and hauled up a part of our house logs during the cool of the morning.

The coach came along this evening but brought no mail for us. The messenger gave us a Denver paper, but there is no particular news.

As we naturally begin to look forward to the time of our discharge we also naturally begin to talk about what it is best to go at when that time comes. Various are the conflicting opinions, and strong the arguments. Verry few have actually made up their minds. Probably a few will go home, some to Bannack, some to Mexico, and a good many remain in Colorado.

### May 19

We hauled the balance of our house logs this morning and this evening we built it up nearley to the proper highth. One of the boys found an order from the War department, in the paper, for the discharge of all cavalry troops whose time expires by the 1st of Oct', and Frazier has borrowed Done's horse and gone to camp to ask the Lieutenant about it.

### May 20

Finished hauling the timber for our house, roofing and so on, this morning, and finished building it this evening, putting on part of the roofing, or rather the poles which form the foundation of the roof. We have built our house about ten feet from the cookhouse, and intend to roof over the space. Frazier came back, and sais the Lieutenant told him he would send for him when he was wanted. He sent a letter by him to Seargent Bryant, saying that he must not let any of the men go up to camp on private business, withhout an order for him

### May 23

Ah! My little book, I have sadly neglected thee of late. I acknowledge that I have been sadley remiss; dillitory, or, to speak more planely, lazy. I ask your forgiveness, and promise to endeavor, to fill up such of them as have been allready passed over, with such thoughts as I may happen to be possessed of from time to time, allways provided your good genious will attend me, and assist in manupulating them into words and sentences.

Washed my shirts this morning

### May 24

We have had some wind and dust today, and it blew through our cabbin most uncerrimoniously

Harpham and I rigged a blanket on the skiff and took a sail. 'Twas something like riding down hill and then having to haul the sled back again, as we could sail onley in one direction, and row back.

Redding came down from camp this evening, and brings the news that Jef Davis is captured!

Ha! That winds it up!

We will surely get our discharge now shortly.

## May 25

The coach came in this p.m. and found us as eager as ever for news. I got a letter from mother. The news of the capture of old Jeff is not confirmed. We got no paper. Sweeney is allmost ready to go crazy becaus his Denver paper does'nt come.

Bryant got an order from Lieutenant Maurril[151] to send me to camp with my effects by the hay train when it comes up

## May 26

Weather still warm, river still high. Major Wincoop[152] with his escort passed down, and camped here for dinner. Jeff is captured. Ed. Stewart came up this afternoon and brought a Denver paper from Bents F't which gives full particulars. The hay train came up this evening and camped here for the night. I suppose private Ostrander with his effects will have to leave in the morning. I dont know what they are going to do with me but conjcature that I am to be sent to A Co.

## May 27

One of the train boys awoke me, as I had requested him, and I got my "effects" togather; took a cold bite for breakfast, helped Nelson[153] who is sick, to get into one of the waggons, bid good bye to the three or four boys who were up, and was off.

Arrived at camp Fillmore about two, and going to the Lieutenant's tent I gave the salute and reported. The Lieutenant told me to go to Denver by the same train and report to the Adg't Gen'l.

Saw the Waggon Boss who says he will not start 'till monday.

Jake and Ellick are here with a waggon load of merchandise

## May 28

Have been lying about camp chatting with the boys, all day: as I am ordered away, and supposed to be with the train on the road, I escaped the inspection which the other boys had to go through. The boys say that Murril is getting more and more millitary every day. They say that he does not allow a private to speak to him except through a noncomissoned officer. Fears are entertained that he will burst some of these fine days, or disappear through the clouds. I suppose it is well enough for him to maintain all the dignity possible now, for a few months, for in all probabillity it would be longer than that before he will be nothing but a man.

## May 29

Picked up my traps, drew ten days rations, and reported myself to Jerrie's train again for transportation to Denver; with an order in my pocket to report to the Ag't Gen. at H'd Qr's

We got started about noon and traviled only about six miles before we camped; which we did on the Arkansas by the side of an asacie[154] at the beginning of the cutoff.

I took a bucket and Boston going with me we went about ¾ of a mile back into the field to a house where I bought a pale full of buttermilk for 50 cts. Noticed several copies of the Crisis pasted upon the walls. Shot a rabbit on the way back. Good bye!!

## May 30

We pulled out of camp a half hour after sunrise this morning, and taking the cutoff traviled about twenty three or four miles, camping on the fountain' about seven miles above the junction of the cutoff with this road, and the side of an asacie across which the mules were driven where there is verry good grass and a good many weedes.

Arrived in camp about 2 p.m. and it comenced raining about four, continuing about an hour

## May 31

Pulled out about sunrise and traviled till about four Oclock, taking the right hand road over the bluffs about twelve miles below Colorado city

The grass is verry good all along the road since we left the Fountain, and the road is also verry good. It comenced raining again about two and continued untill we got into camp which we have made at a gap through the hills where the road from Colorado city joins this.

Verry good watter and grass, pleanty of pine wood on the hills. Another light shower after ariving in camp. Found where somebody has camped on the verry top of a high hill.

### June 1

Me and my bunkey Douning, an old acquantance of my last trip across the planes, got up and put our bed into a waggon, in order to get out of the rain, and consequently did'n't get wakened up before breakfast.

We awoke just after the grub and mess kit had been packed away in the waggon, and had to "dig" it out again. The train got on the road a little before sunrise, good road pleanty of water and grass. Camped about noon at a ranche on the divide, where the boys not onley found pleanty of good grass for their mules, but an abundance of excellent hay for them to lay to after being tied up

### June 2

Started about sunrise and travailed over a rather unfrequented, but verry excellent road in about directly a northern direction, about twenty-two miles, to near Richison's where we camped.

### June 3

Got started earley enough to reach the top of the hill just as the sun was showing his genial face over the hills in the direction of the stamping grounds of the cowardly Cheyennes. Away to the north could be seene the low range of the Black hills, and nearer the towring and glistning Long's Peak, amid a gallaxy of lesser peaks, all flashing back the first ray of the morning sun from their snowtipped sumets, while still nearer winds a black line across the foreground; the line of the platt, on whose bank is vissable a cluster of white specks, the city of Denver 25 miles distant

### June 4

We arrived in town about two oclock yesterday and I went immediately and reported to the Ag't Gen'l, whom I find instead of being the foppish little whiffit I had looked for, is nothing more than a man and a perfectly gentlemanly appearing one at that.

He gave me a pass 'till four and told me to report again at that time. I did so, and got an order to report to the comanding officer of A Co. at Junction station. I found a stopping place at the Bennet house, and have been loafing about from one place to another all day, with some of the old boys who been discharged.

### June 5

Have seene Seargent Skinner[155] of G Co, who is up from Living Springs with some Co teams, and is going back tommorraw.

As that is in my direction, I am going out with him. Been loafing about with Ben and George, and some of the other boys. Find it as dull business as ever, I allways considered it the hardest kind of Work.

Business is tolerable brisk appaarantly, but not as much so as I had expected to find it

### June 6

Seargent Skinner told me this morning to be ready to start at one oclock. I went to the Provost Marshalls office and got my ration return and then to the Commissary and drew six days rations. There is just about enough to fill my hat, of flour, bacon, beanes, coffee, and sugar.

Waited for Skinner untill about three, and had begun to think he was not coming today, when he came and we got off.

It comenced to rain just as we got started, and continued 'till night.

We came about fourteene miles to cole creek, and are all as wet as drowned rats

Took a square meal of bread, butter, and milk.

### June 7

Got out of a wet bed, put on wet cloths, fussed around 'till nine oclock before we got our breakfast, put wet harnesses, on to wet mules, and fineally got off

One of the boys receipted for forage which we never got, to pay for our supper and breakfast. It has rained the biggest share of the day, and as we were wet yesterday, and if possable wetter last night, we are wettest tonight.

We drove thirty five miles by about three oclock and arrived at living springs, at the camp of Co G.

Every thing is afloat, and everybody wet. I got a cup of beane soupe, and a hunk of bread for supper

### June 8

I had a dry bed to sleepe in last night, and got some warm coffee for breakfast. Found three ambulances here going below and got a ride down to the Junction which is about forty miles.

We got started about eight and came through by about three. I reported to Lieut' Quinby[156] who is in command of the Co. I find a good many of my old acquaintances here.

Winches, McCoune, Stewart,[157] and one of the recruits of old Co F are here, and a good many of my acquaintances of old K also

### June 9

Dr. Yates asked me if I would be willing to go on daily duty to look after the sick men in camp. I told him I was ready to do any duty which I could stand

Accordingly Lieut' Quinby ordered me to report to Dr. Yates this afternoon, and I did so.

There are but three sick in our camp and they do not need much care; consequently I have it rather light at present.

In fact I find it rather "a soft snap"

The clouds have cleared away, and El Sol is out again in all his glory

### June 10

The Sun shines bright and pleasant, but the weather is not disagreeably warm

I had to dress Bubes leg bring the medison for McDonald and thats about all I have done

### June 13

The Dr. is going away on the coach to Denver tonight and he says I will have to get along as well as I can by myself. There are oneley about a dozzen on sick report, and they are none of them likely to die right off.

Yates has been giving me instructions about what to do with them. A pleasant day but verry little to do: consequently it is rather dull

### June 14

Pleasant weather and warm enough

Am sorely bothered about What to do with some of these sick fellows. Hav prescribed rest for the most of them

### June 15

This being Doctor, Steward and nurse, is rather heavy for a private.

Some of the troops here are what *we* call galvanized yankees. They suppose me to be some new Doctor who has relieved Yates.

There are several new caces this morning, but the most of them are either scruvy or diarhea. One has fever. I have given them a few simple medicins, such as I know the Dr. would give in the same caces and ordered rest. The fact is these fellows have been shamefully abused, having been marched on foot across the planes, with scanty clothing and poor rations, and they all need rest and vegetables too.

### June 16

The sky has been pretty cloudy all day, and they became so heavy in the afternoon as to drop a few sprinkles of rain. Another big train (two hundred waggons) passed this afternoon.

Most of them contained families, and the most of the families are south-ern people going to oragon and Idaho

Am getting along as well as I could wish: onley two new cases, and those verry simple ones

### June 17

I am getting along fully with the boy that has the fever. If I had some-thing better for him to eat I should like it better. Coffee bread and bacon are hardly the thing for a sick man.

A man came here for a doctor to attend a man in a passing train. There is no Dr. here so I had to go.

I found the man with a ball in his Shoulder, and his wife with a flesh wound in her arm from the same ball.

I dare not undertake to extract the ball, or set the broken bones. I saw that neither was likely to bleed to death, 'though the man spit blood and suffered considerably. I could only give them some dressing, a few dose of morphia and advise them to reach denver as soon as possible

### June 18

These galvanised boys call me Dr. and salute me when they see me pass-ing, which makes me ashamed of myself. Some of our boys are beginining to bore me by calling me Dock too. I don't care Yates don't come and I'm going to do the best I can.

### June 19

Well I'll be darned if this Dock' business aint getting pretty heavy

Had another call from cittizens again today.

A small child had been run over by a loaded waggon: the wheele passed across his bowells as he lay upon his back. Found there were no bones broken. He was spitting blood and in great pain. didn't know what *to* do, but fineally, gave him a dose of castor oil, and a few doses of morphia with advice to go to denver. The train was bound for Montana

### *June 20*

A whole new batch of these galvanised boys came at sick call. I reported some of the old ones for duty and took up a lot more on sick report

It wont do to send them off without some kind of medicin, and as some of them do not seeme to have much the matter with them It's hard to tell what to give them.

The scurvy caces I give citric acid. One fellow I gave a few powders of S't Louis flour

Ill be d—d if I'm going to [be] giving minerals[158] unless I *know* I am right

### *June 21*

A warm sultry day! Verry little air stirring and no clouds untill near night, when a heavy bank of clouds came up and graduly filled the heavens, with the exception of a small patch of clear sky in the north east

### *June 22*

Sent some more of them to duty. my flour patient is well. shouldn't have taken him on sick report but didn't know but he *might* be sick

The *Dr.* has to take *their* word for it sometimes.

### *June 23*

I believe I've got this fever case all right now. He dont appear to have aney fever today and I have given him a tonic

He hasent been verry low at no time

### *June 24*

Rather cool during the fore part of the day, but quite Warm in the after part. I have been doing verry little all day, and the most of what I did do has been of the listless loafing sort, and consisted mostly in hanging about the ranche and camp

Prescribed blue mass Salts oil[159] and rest to a few more of the sick lame and lazy fellows

### June 25

Dr. Yates came back by the last nights coach and was here to see to the sick call himself, which relieved me of a load of responsabiltiy

I was getting considerably pusseled [puzzled] about some of these cases, though the most of them I got along with well enough as they were just such as I have before seene treated. The Dr. looked over the prascription book and expressed himself well satisfied with my treatment

### October 1

Well I have got to come to it and do my regular cook.

I had scarcely got settled when I was dilated for cook and had to go to work this morning.

I have had another negligent streak and it has lasted a good while this time, and I don't know as I shall ever redeeme myself again as a diary keeper.

Sometimes perhaps when I feel like it I shall write a line or two

### October 2

The news of the day is that the Vet Batt 1st Col. Cav are to be mustered out forth with. Of course it won't be done untill we are relieved here

### October 4

There have been sent a set of muster out rolls to the cos. here, and the news is that some Missouri Cav. are enroute from denver to relieve us.

### October 10

The cavalry have arrived at last. There are three Cos. of them and they are camped on the bottom opposite the post and I suppose that now we will be relieved shortly or sooner.

### November 3

Well here I come again to make a mark or two after so long a time.

I am a cittizen now was mustered out just one week ago and am now in a cabbin near the platt canion writing a little while Jim Hall Killmore, Winches and McCime are playing a game of seven up. Us five are here cutting wood by the cord. Bill and I have been here two days and I am as sore as a worn out cavalry horse. Work foes [goes] mighty hard after so long a time of soldering

It seemes odd to be a free man once more

*November 5*

Went down the gulch a mile and a half and helped to grind the axes have made a verry dull day of it. There are no accomudations here at all scarcely. there are no chairs or table; We sleep on the ground, the chimney smokes and there is nobody in particular to cook. There are four of Rollinses hands here and they all profess to know nothing about cooking. We'll have to stand it I recon 'till we get the wood cut below and build a cabbin of our own

*November 9*

Nothing to eat but Bread bacon and cofee without sugar. All hands are mad becaus Ned. Rollins has not brought up some grub. We did nothing but fugle around all the fore noon. guess we will chop a little this afternoon

*December 11*

Snow, snow, till you cant rest!

Well! Thank the Lord we have a good cabbin and pleantly to eat. It cammensed to snow last night at dark, and had covered the ground to the depth of six inches at daylight and still continues. It's ten Oclock, snow still falling, and two of the boys have gone hunting

2 Oclock! John came in with a fine deer and says Bill. is on the track of another

5½ Oclock! Bill came in and says he wounded one but couldn't get him.

*December 12*

Today Jim Hall and I have been out hunting. I got on the track of some but did not come up with them. Jim got on track and followed up till he saw his deer but did not get a shot.

Both tired and hungry but no deer

The other boys laugh at us.

Has snowed a fine meager misty snow nearly all day

*December 13*

John and Bill went out again today, and were gone nearley all day. They report no fresh tracks seene, but those of Mountain Lyon, or Couger. Their tracks are to be seene all through the mountains Here. One was seene a quarter of a mile up the gulch the other day feeding upon the remains of a blacktail which he had evidently killed. The man who saw him was afraid to shoot as he had but one load, and feared he might miss his aim.

A verry cold day! The air full of a frozen mist.

The boys came in with their whiskers and mustachoes covered with frost and ice.

## December 14

We have all been housed up in the cabbin, mending clothes, spinning yarnes cracking jokes, etc, all day

Weather a degree or two milder

## December 15

Bill John and I are going hunting across the river and don't expect to get back 'till tomorrow night

## December 16

We got in this evening, Verry tired and verry hungry

Did'nt kill anything but two days of time

Bill saw some deere and John and I saw their tracks. I took a tract and followed it 'till dark, yesterday, and expected to have to camp out alone supperless, but the boys got on my tract and overtook me a little befor dark.

We built fires and kept tolerable warm but did'nt sleep much.

Rather up hill business where the most of the ground lays at an angle of 45 degrees or over. Saw pleanty of Lyon tracks

## December 17

Jim and McC, have gone to town to see if they can raise anything out of Ed. Rollins

John Bill and myself have been making ourselves as comfortable as possible all day. We feele the want of reading matter

## December 18

Bill, John and I have been cutting some oak wood.

The air is verry frosty, full of mist which gathers and freeses upon everything

## December 19

We went to work last evening to build a sled, which we finished this morning; and Bill and John went down to Old Wakeman and got some hay this afternoon.

Weather milder

*December 20*

Have been just fugleing about and looking for Jim, & McC to come in.

Made out to get a few old logs thrown to gather some where near in the shape of a stable for the horses

The boys came in about dark

News unimportant

*December 21*

Ed Rollins came in and measured out wood today! We have cut in all 512 cords and it will amount to over $650.00

Some of the boys are going down with Ed. to get as much of it as possible

*December 22*

The boys are all gone and I am left here alone.

McCune will go to the states, Jim Hall is going to look for a job, but I expect Bill, & John will come back as soon as they can

Rebell Jim. came along and stopped here with me all day.

We have been talking about the war, etc, etc;

*December 23*

Illinois Jim came along this morning and Rebell Jim went out to help him hunt the cattle. I expect Rebell Jim will come back to stay with me tonight

Mighty lonesome!!!

*December 24*

All alone again! Jim has gone for good this time. I am in hopes John or Bill, or both will get back this evening, Hope they'l find some kind of a job for to make something at.

This wood cutting job has not turned out verry well: it played out too soon.

We could have done verry wel had it lasted all winter as we expected.

As it is we had oneley just got farely settled down, when Ed. Rollins gets short of funds and we will have to quit.

Have been here nearly two months, and have only made about a hundred dollars a piece and a'int sure of getting that right away. Have spent nearly all my money, and now no means of making more at present.

*December 25*

A lonely Christmas this for me!! Nobody to keep me company but the dogs Jack & Peter Hurdle! It has been snowing all day and has covered the ground to the depth of about a foot.

Have got pleanty to eat such as it is, and its good enough what there is of it. Neither Bill. or John appear to get back somehow.

This Crusoish life is'nt verry interesting in practice however much so it may be to read about

Have been reading a little from Thomas De Quincy this evening

Would like to read all his works!

*December 26*

Still alone! Pleanty of snow, and pleanty of sunshine. Shoveled the snow off the roof after breakfast for passtime. Hope the boys will get back tonight.

Four Oclock! No boys yet! Cut pleanty of wood, built a big fire, and am looking! So's Jack looking! So's Pete!

Five! Got my old horse into the stable, and fed him some hay! We're all hands still looking up the gulch

Don't see anything in particular! Begin to fear we wo'nt!

Nine! Been reading Thomas De Quincy! Have read it before! Guess I'll go to bed!

Ten! Got up and punched the fire, and broiled some venison. Will try the bed again.

*December 27*

Have just finished my Breakfast, and fed the dogs, and am now taking my regular smoke. It's half past ten. Not verry early rising to be sure! But What time is spent in bed, is done with anyhow

I'll be darned if I don't begin to think this is pretty heavy on me! The boys were to be back in three or four days *sure*, and here it is the sixth day, and "I'm left all alone" yet. But I presume they will explane all when they come tonight.

*December 28*

Well! John came in last night with Bill's team. He says they could get nothing out of Ed. Rollins, but Bill has stayed behind to try and get a couple of yoke of Rawlins' cattle and we are going to take a yoke which he has running here.

We took the Horses and sled and went down to old Wakemans and got some hay. I came up with it and John stayed behind to hunt the cattle

Half past five! He has'nt come yet, and I have had supper ready and waiting for half an hour

*December 29*

Bill got in last night after John and I had gone to bed. He brought one yoke of cattle.

John didn't find the speckled cattle yesterday, and he has gone to hunt them again today and has not got back yet at 7½ Oclock

*December 30*

John didn't get back last night!

Bill and I went to hauling oak wood down the hill on the sled. I drove and by some means I go [got] the mare hurt on the glifle[160] joint so she will not be able to work again for some time. It seemes that we are having an awfull streak of hard luck all at once. out of money nearly out of grub, tried to haul some wood to get some grub with and now the team laid up and I the unfotunate caus

*December 31*

Bill started to hunt the cattle, as John came in last night without having found them, and John and I went to work to make a wood rack with which I am to start to town with a load of oak to get some groceries with

About the first motion I went to work and cut my foot. John has taken the cattle down to ranche. I don't know what we *will* do!

It seemes that all our bad luck come through me lately, and all at once. We've all three got the blues!

Bill has just come in but did'nt find the cattle. Rather an unpropitious winding up of the year! We'll start anew tomorrow

*Found by Chas. E Vest 1922—Eagle Warehouse, Fresno California*

# Notes

[1] A ranch on the Santa Fe Trail east of Apache Canyon and just east of Glorieta Pass.

[2] Pvt. William L. Mencer, Company F. The roster of the First Colorado Cavalry comes from Ovando J. Hollister's *Boldly They Rode: A History of the First Colorado Regiment of Volunteers* (Lakewood, Colo.: Golden Press, 1949; originally published 1863).

[3] Pvt. George W. Lowe, Company F.

[4] Fort Lyon was a U.S. Army post in southeast Colorado on the Santa Fe Trail near the site of Bent's Old Fort. Originally known as Bent's New Fort, which the trader William Bent constructed farther east on the Arkansas River, it became Fort Wise in 1860, then was renamed in honor of Union General Nathaniel Lyons, killed in Missouri in 1861. The army moved the fort to a new site in 1867.

[5] Lt. George Nelson, resigned August 31, 1862.

[6] Ostrander is probably referring to his Sharp's carbine. Records as to the type of weapons carried are sketchy. According to Frederick Todd's *American Military Equipage, 1851–1872*, the primary armament of the First Colorado Cavalry in 1862 included an 1841 rifle (.41 cal.), 1847 musketoon (rifled), some Sharp's carbines, 1855 rifled muskets, Colt Army revolvers, Colt Navy revolvers, Whitney Navy revolvers. The army issued additional weapon types in 1864 to the First Colorado.

[7] San Jose is a settlement near the site of Glorieta Pass.

[8] Refers to Apache Canyon near the site of Glorieta Pass.

[9] Refers to the village of Tichalote, near Las Vegas, New Mexico.

[10] Walker was the commander of the U.S. Third Cavalry at the battle of Glorieta Pass.

[11] A settlement in northeastern New Mexico.

[12] Col. John Slough, commander of the Union forces against Lt. Col. William Read Scurry, CSA, at the battle of Glorieta Pass.

[13] Fountaineque or Fountain qui Bouille, south of present-day Colorado Springs. Now known as Fountain Creek.

[14] Fort Union was a garrison in northeast New Mexico.

[15] A sutler sold supplies to soldiers.

[16] Camp Weld, aka Fort Weld, aka Camp Elbert. A military post in Arapahoe County, now a part of Denver.

[17] Original name of present-day Golden, Colorado.

[18] Capt. Samuel H. Cook, Company F.

[19] Pvt. Theo M. Shearer, Company F.

[20] Sgt. George Gardner, Quartermaster, Company A.

[21] 3rd Duty Sgt. Jesse F. Keel, Company F.

[22] 1st Cpl. J. M. Blakey, Company D.

[23] Typical pay for privates was $13.00 per month according to Don Rickey, Jr.'s, *Forty Miles a Day on Beans and Hay: The Enlisted Soldier Fighting the Indian Wars.*

[24] Pvt. William D. Kilmore and 3rd Corporal James A. Boles, Company F.

[25] Pvt. Adam Pritchard, Company F.

[26] A military post in south-central Colorado in the San Luis Valley on Sangre de Cristo Creek. Established in 1858 to protect settlers from Indian attack, it briefly was under the command of Kit Carson and was home to numerous army units, including the Buffalo Soldiers after the Civil War.

[27] Cache la Poudre River, a tributary of the South Platte River.

[28] Adjutant 1st Lt. George H. Stilwell.

[29] Territorial officials Governor John Evans (1862–65), Secretary Samuel H. Elbert (1862–66), Attorney Samuel E. Browne (1862–65), and General John Chivington, commander of the First Cavalry of Colorado. Ostrander apparently did not hear the secretary's name clearly.

[30] 1st Lt. John C. Anderson, quartermaster on Chivington's staff of the First Colorado Cavalry.

[31] Cañon City, a settlement south and west of Colorado City.

[32] Pvt. Charles D. Wendell, Company F.

[33] 1st Cpl. John Ferris, Company F.

[34] According to Don Rickey, Jr., author of *Forty Miles a Day on Beans and Hay: The Enlisted Soldier Fighting the Indian Wars*, a day's marching ration was 1 lb. of hard crackers (about ten), ¾ lb. salt pork, 1¼ oz. coffee, and about 3 oz. sugar per man.

[35] General John M. Chivington, hero of the battle of Glorieta Pass.

[36] The original name for Colorado Springs.

[37] Commander of the Second Colorado Cavalry.

[38] Pvt. Thomas Allen, Company F.

[39] A mining settlement near Central City.

[40] Barthalomew F. Foley, bugler, Company F.

[41] 1st Lt. Luther Wilson, Company F, and 2nd Lt. John Oster, Jr., Company K.

[42] Travelers generally gauged distance in two ways: they had a pretty good idea how far they could travel in a given time by horse; and the trails, while not marked, were traveled enough that they knew how far it was from one major landmark to another.

[43] Tarryall was a settlement northeast of Fairplay, near Hamilton. The Tarryall Road connected Cañon City to Tarryall.

[44] Kenosha House was a way station northeast of Fairplay and at the east (Kenosha Pass) side of South Park, on the Old South Park Stage Road.

[45] Mountain park in central Colorado Rocky Mountains.

[46] Mining settlement in South Park.

[47] Buffalo Springs was a mining settlement due south of Fairplay.

[48] Pvt. Charles E. Strope, Company F.

[49] Major river flowing southeast from the Rockies across southeast Colorado.

[50] Pvt. James H. Tantum, Company F.

[51] A mining camp northwest of Fairplay.

[52] The so-called "French ranch," owned by Adolph Guiraud (or Guireaud) in South Park.

[53] Pvt. John Hawkins, Company I.

[54] Daniel McLaughlin operated a way station on the Denver–South Park stagecoach road. His ranch was located near the present site of Como, some ten miles northeast of Fairplay.

[55] Original mining camp on site of what became Leadville, Colorado, in 1879.

[56] Pvt. John Winches, Company F.

[57] Herriman and his wife were the proprietors of Kenosha House. See note 44.

[58] Pvt. David Rice, Company E.

[59] Another way station kept by Daniel McLaughlin.

[60] A settlement northeast of Fairplay.

[61] Slat's Ranch, on the Old South Park Stage Road northeast of Fairplay.

[62] 1st Duty Sgt. Alex. Cochran, Company F.

[63] The fact that Ostrander still refers to the "guerillas" rather than the Espinosas indicates the preoccupation the troops had with Confederate invaders.

[64] Tributary of the Arkansas in South Park.

[65] Pvt. Horatio H. Babcock, Company F.

[66] Pvt. Samuel G. Johns, Company E.

[67] According to Rickey's *Forty Miles a Day on Beans and Hay*, poker was popular with enlisted men, especially stud and draw poker, and seven-up and high-low-jack. Even though all forms of gambling were considered illegal, the army did not enforce the regulation.

[68] Tributary of the Arkansas in South Park.

[69] Initially established by Ohio Republicans in 1862 in response to the Copperheads, the Union leagues formed to support the war effort following early Union losses, and to revitalize the Republican Party. They also served as social organizations. In the postwar South, leagues formed to promote the Republican cause among free blacks.

[70] Presumably Pvt. James Stevens, Company F.

[71] Pvt. John S. Kirkpatrick, Company K.

[72] 4th Cpl. John V. Webber, Company F.

[73] A Denver boardinghouse.

[74] A poker game. In this form, players buy in at the beginning and after losing all their chips are out of the game.

[75] Pvt. James Hall, Company F.

[76] St. Vrain Creek, a tributary of the South Platte River, northeast of Denver.

[77] The Big Thompson Creek, a tributary of the South Platte, northeast of Denver.

[78] Site of present-day Fort Collins.

[79] Boxelder Creek, a tributary of the South Platte River.

[80] Fort Walbach, near Cheyenne Pass in southeastern Wyoming.

[81] Chugwater Creek, a tributary of the Laramie River in southeastern Wyoming.

[82] Presumably Fort Laramie in southeastern Wyoming.

[83] Near Whisky Gap, Wyoming.

[84] Probably Horse Tail Creek in northeast Colorado, a tributary of the South Platte.

[85] A settlement northwest of present-day Fort Collins, Colorado.

[86] A settlement that had been called La Porte.

[87] Pvt. Justin W. Crittenden, Company M.

[88] Refers to the reservation of the Cheyenne and the Arapaho tribes in southeast Colorado.

[89] Bent's Old Fort was a trading post along the Santa Fe Trail, on the Arkansas River, near present La Junta, Colorado. Charles Bent (1799–1847), his brother William (1809–69), Cerán St. Vrain (1798–1870), and their associates built the fort in 1833. In 1849 William, then sole owner, blew it up after failing to sell it to the government for a sufficient sum. William later built Bent's New Fort farther downstream and leased it to the government in 1859.

[90] Pvt. John McCormick, Company F.

[91] Probably William Bent.

[92] 7th Cpl. Alfred D. Ruyle, Company F.

[93] Pvt. Adam Pritchard, Pvt. William D. Kilmore, and Pvt. George Ayres, Company F.

[94] Major Scott J. Anthony, 1st Colorado Cavalry.

[95] Pvt. Valentine P. Buchanan and Pvt. Benjamin F. Ferris, Company F.

[96] 5th Duty Sgt. John E. Jones, Company F.

[97] Probably means the Santa Fe Trail.

[98] Pvt. James Hall, Company F.

[99] Pvt. Eli H. More, Company F.

[100] 1st Lt. Luther Wilson, Company F. Appears that Ostrander erred on Wilson's rank.

[101] Pvt. Hiram M. Springer, Company F.

[102] Likely a reference to the issued ration of whisky, which was equal to one gill or four ounces.

[103] 5th Duty Sgt. John E. Jones, Company F.

[104] 2nd Lt. Solon N. Ackley, Company F.

[105] Pvt. Michael Hollenbeck, Company F.

[106] It is not clear what Ostrander means by "a card of bread."

[107] Maj. Jacob Downing, First Cavalry of Colorado.

[108] Ostrander seldom identifies people by their first name. Tomey is presumably Pvt. Thomas "Tommy" Allen, Company F.

[109] Pvt. Alfred Frazier, Company F.

[110] Pvt. Rhoderick F. Harper, Company F.

[111] Pvt. George W. Pierce, Company F.

[112] Cpl. James A. Boles, Company F.

[113] As mentioned in the Preface, Ostrander concluded the first diary with a letter to his mother, written in February 1864.

[114] Led the First Colorado Cavalry in the building of Fort Lyon in 1860.

[115] On north bank, looking east down the river.

[116] Explorer John Charles Frémont.

[117] The original name for Fort Lyon. The name was changed June 25, 1862, because Wise was a Confederate.

[118] The Purgatoire River, which empties into the Arkansas River about forty miles east of Pueblo.

[119] It is unclear who this is.

[120] It is unclear whom Ostrander means here. There were two Private Youngs, neither named Tom, and no one with the name of Bonser.

[121] Cribbage is a popular card game usually played with a board and pegs to count scoring.

[122] Ostrander seems to be referencing King Adherbal, who once ruled Numidia.

[123] Masked battery, a reference to a hidden battery of artillery.

[124] A reference to the Colorado Third, the militia led by John Chivington in the attack at Sand Creek. It appears that Ostrander and others shared Cpt. Silas Soule's disgust for the unit.

[125] Maj. Samuel M. Logan, previously captain of Company B.

[126] Means Julesburg, a settlement in northeast corner of Colorado.

[127] Site of present-day Fort Morgan, Colorado.

[128] A reference to Uncle Sam, that is, the government.

[129] Pvt. John A. Gallagher and Pvt. George Cassidy, Company F.

[130] Frantz Metzler, bugler, Company F.

[131] Pvt. William R. Beattie, Company F.

[132] Revolver battery.

[133] Pvt. George Cassidy and Pvt. Fayette Place, Company F.

[134] Pvt. Thomas R. Cox, Company D.

[135] Pvt. Frank Holmes, Company F.

[136] Ostrander's handwriting is not clear; this appears to be Pvt. William Lambdon, Company E.

[137] Lawrence, Kansas.

[138] Pvt. George W. Lowe, Company F.

[139] Capt. Silas Soule, the commander of the regular army troops at the Sand Creek Massacre who defied Chivington and refused to commit his men to the slaughter; was later shot dead on the streets of Denver.

[140] 1st Lt. Luther Wilson, Company F.

[141] 1st Sgt. John C. Turner, Company C.

[142] 1st Lt. James Olney, who had been promoted in the field from 4th Duty Sgt., Company A.

[143] A more direct route from the trail along the South Platte southwest across Bijou and Kiowa creeks to Denver.

[144] Pvt. Samuel Lewis, 3rd Cpl. James A. Boles, 4th Cpl. John V. Webber, and Pvt. Alfred Frazier, all of Company F.

[145] Pvt. David K. Bailey, Company F.

[146] 1st Duty Sgt. Alex. Cochran and Pvt. Alexander Monarque, previously of Company F.

[147] Either Cpl. R. Bruce McGahey or Cpl. John T. McGahey, Company F. One had been promoted from private.

[148] Pvt. William Mencer, Company F.

[149] Pvt. John H. Harpham, Company M.

[150] Company Sergeant Al. T. Randall, Company H.

[151] Probably Frank Murrell, who had been 2nd lieutenant of Company B.

[152] Maj. Edward W. Wynkoop, First Cavalry of Colorado.

[153] Probably Pvt. Nis Nelson, Company L.

[154] An *acequia*, Spanish for irrigation ditch.

[155] Most likely Sgt. David C. Skinner, Company G, who had received a field promotion.

[156] 2nd Lt. Ira Quimby, Company M.

[157] Pvt. John Winces; Pvt. Chancellor McCune, Company F; and Pvt. John Stewart, Company M.

[158] The most common "minerals" used were arsenic and mercury compounds.

[159] A mercury compound.

[160] Handwriting is unclear, but Ostrander is likely referring to the knee joint.

# Index